PRAI

SEEKING SERENITY

"Amanda Enayati takes us to the intersection of science, philosophy, and spirituality in order to create a road map for not only surviving, but thriving in a world fueled by stress and burnout. Her extensive research, years of reporting, and compelling firsthand accounts give *Seeking Serenity* the power to change the conversation and help us live our lives with less stress and more fulfillment."

—Arianna Huffington, *New York Times* bestselling author of *Thrive*

"*Seeking Serenity* is a big-picture look at what stress is trying to tell us about how to live better, happier, and healthier lives. It's a much-needed antidote to an increasingly stressful world."

—Charles Duhigg, Pulitzer Prize–winning reporter and *New York Times* bestselling author of the *The Power of Habit*

"*Seeking Serenity* is an indispensable guide to these difficult times. Amanda Enayati's experiences of exile, illness, and parenthood make it real and essential. A journalist who stumbled into the field of stress management—she does an inspiring job of teaching us how to calm down and live happily."

—Erica Jong, international bestselling author of *Fear of Flying*

SEEKING SERENITY

THE 10 NEW RULES
FOR HEALTH AND HAPPINESS
IN THE AGE OF ANXIETY

AMANDA ENAYATI

NEW AMERICAN LIBRARY

NEW AMERICAN LIBRARY
Published by New American Library,
an imprint of Penguin Random House LLC
375 Hudson Street, New York, New York 10014

This book is a publication of New American Library. Previously published in a
New American Library hardcover edition.

First New American Library Trade Paperback Printing, January 2016

For more information about Penguin Random House, visit penguin.com.

NEW AMERICAN LIBRARY TRADE PAPERBACK ISBN: 978-0-451-47227-4

THE LIBRARY OF CONGRESS HAS CATALOGED THE HARDCOVER EDITION OF THIS TITLE AS FOLLOWS:

Enayati, Amanda.
Seeking serenity: the 10 new rules for health and happiness in the age of anxiety/Amanda Enayati.
p. cm.
ISBN 978-0-451-47151-2 (hardback)
1. Stress (Psychology)   2. Stress management.   3. Mental health.
4. Well-being.   5. Inner peace.   I. Title.
BF575.S75E53 2015
155.9'042—dc23 2014029563

Printed in the United States of America
10 9 8 7 6 5 4 3 2 1

Designed by Elke Sigal

PUBLISHER'S NOTE
While the author has made every effort to provide accurate telephone numbers, Internet addresses and other
contact information at the time of publication, neither the publisher nor the author assumes any responsibility for errors, or for changes that occur after publication. Further, publisher does not have any control over
and does not assume any responsibility for author or third-party Web sites or their content.

Penguin
Random
House

To Mina and Rohan,
I hope you dance.

CONTENTS

"Real isn't how you are made," said the Skin Horse. "It's a thing that happens to you . . ."

"Does it hurt?" asked the Rabbit.

"Sometimes," said the Skin Horse, for he was always truthful. "When you are Real you don't mind being hurt."

"Does it happen all at once, like being wound up," he asked, "or bit by bit?"

"It doesn't happen all at once," said the Skin Horse. "You become. It takes a long time. That's why it doesn't happen often to people who break easily, or have sharp edges, or who have to be carefully kept. Generally, by the time you are Real, most of your hair has been loved off, and your eyes drop out and you get loose in the joints and very shabby. But these things don't matter at all, because once you are Real you can't be ugly, except to people who don't understand."

—**Margery Williams**, *The Velveteen Rabbit*

The Stressed Columnist

People often chuckle when I tell them I am a stress columnist. I will grant that it is an odd title, but the job itself—examining stress and its impacts—has become crucial in modern life.

My journey into the stress vortex began in late 2010 when I wrote two series of essays for CNN.com: one about the milestones of my brawl with cancer and the other about parenting toddlers in the wake of a health crisis. A few months after the latter, Mary Carter, who ran CNN Health in those days, asked me to give her a call.

"We are going back to the basics," she told me. "We have sex and sleep covered. I need you to write about stress."

Stress.

Her suggestion blindsided me. I was, in spite of my relative youth, already an old pro at full-catastrophe living—that is, constant disaster punctuated by brief periods of quiet. Because of this, stress was my default; it was the "normal" I accepted as status quo and not something to be questioned. The idea of exploring stress, writing about it and finding ways to manage and alleviate it, seemed strange. I was also far more interested in writing about other health topics. Three years out from a scrape with death, I had a bone to pick with our culture's very linear way of thinking about health and illness.

"I want you to take our readers into the stress vortex," she continued. "People are half out of their minds with stress. Tell them how to help themselves."

I opened my mouth to protest, to tell Mary that I didn't know the first thing about stress.

And then closed it.

This was not strictly true.

I was, in fact, Waldo in the *Where's Waldo* of stressful life circumstances: As a young child, I had been banished from my homeland because of my faith, then virtually orphaned for years in the wake of exile. In my adult life I spent years as a desperately unhappy Big Firm lawyer, someone who was standing in the shadows of the Twin Towers on the day they crumbled, and who suffered a vicious depression afterward. And then, the final insult: late-stage cancer in my thirties. Surgery, six rounds of high-dose chemo and radiation later, the fact that I was still standing was something of a miracle, given the odds of survival I had been quoted three years earlier.

The book of my life was a virtual encyclopedia of disaster. What *didn't* I know about stress?

It was a compelling proposition. I had researched and read reams across a variety of disciplines—science, philosophy, self-help and spirituality—in the wake of my various catastrophes. And all that information and advice resonated, more or less, as I read the books. But it stuck only in the way New Year's resolutions stick—for days, weeks, sometimes months. The clarity was always somehow transient. Eventually it dissipated, and sooner rather than later. Lasting peace proved itself elusive.

In the end, it was the name of the column that clinched the deal for me.

"Seeking Serenity," we decided after volleying several options back and forth. "The quest for well-being and life balance in stressful times."

I remember turning the words over in my head. It was a quest—it said so in the title. No promises.

I can do this, I thought. *I can seek serenity.*

As for the prospect of well-being and life balance in stressful times, was that even possible? If so, I wanted it badly.

It was not until much later that I wondered at the mysterious forces that had set me on this path. All I knew then was that my editor was sending me on an assignment with stress as a road map. Two weeks later I officially entered the stress vortex. It would be the journey of a lifetime.

PART ONE

THE TRUE STORY OF STRESS

One does not discover new lands without consenting
to lose sight of the shore for a very long time.

—ANDRÉ GIDE

PART ONE

THE TRUE STORY OF STRESS

CHAPTER ONE

The Stories We Tell Ourselves

The restaurant is called Café Gratitude. It originated, unsurprisingly, in Northern California. And if the vegan establishment's name doesn't adequately give away its bohemian spirit, the menu puts all doubt to rest.

On a given morning, you might decide to order pancakes.

"I am openhearted," you will say.

Or a bowl of porridge: "I am free."

"I am radiant" begets a mimosa; "I am courageous," a coffee.

The entire menu forms a small universe of affirmations, mantras that you might whisper to yourself (cringing, perhaps) as you decide what you want to eat. Then you will repeat the mantras once again to the server. You may even giggle or blush as you say them out loud.

The idea of ordering food through sunny self-affirmations is rooted in the founders' belief, well established by science, that practicing gratitude in our daily lives is life changing.

But there is something else there too: the fundamental truth that our words matter. That the words we repeat to ourselves over and over again surround us, hypnotize us somehow. They take shape to form our stories, the core of our beliefs, the fabric of our existence.

"Storytelling is the great democracy," National Book Award–winning novelist Colum McCann once told me. "We all want to—need to—tell our stories. There is a certain catharsis in being able to tell your story, in confronting your demons."

But there are stories that serve us. And stories that don't.

What are the stories that you repeat to yourself over and over again? How mindful are you of your unspoken mantras? What are the threads that run through your everyday and, eventually, your entire life?

I am smart.

I am alone.

I am always late.

I am a fake.

Consider this mantra: *I am stressed.*

Think about how many times on any given day you hear some version of it thrown about, whether in casual conversation or grave circumstances. *How stressful! I was stressing hard! He stresses me out!* Or some other variation of the same: *She is so type A.*

How often do we think about stress, repeat its perverse mantra to ourselves, hear it echoed back to us from a diverse array of sources, both public and intimate, both within our heads and without, written, spoken or otherwise signaled? In what ways does stress weave itself into the fabric of our lives?

The View from the Trenches

Nor is all that stress just in our imagination. So many of us feel besieged by what the World Health Organization has referred to as the health epidemic of the twenty-first century. Between 70 to 90 percent of primary care doctors' visits are attributed to stress, which is also said to cost American companies as much as $300 billion a year.[1]

The past few decades have seen increased scientific understanding of stress pathways, the impact of stress on our bodies and minds, and the populations that suffer most from stress and why. Not only have scientists grown highly adept at measuring stress, but soon even the average person on the street will be able to use his smartphone to measure and confirm just how stressed out he might be in real time.[2]

Americans now suffer from an array of diseases that are either rooted in or worsened by stress. We can trace its pernicious impact as the common thread that runs through some of our deadliest public health crises—obesity, diabetes, depression, suicide, cancer, among others. And the sense of pervasive stress has trickled down to the youngest among us, who are mirroring adults' worries, but with far greater consequence and lasting impact.[3]

---

[1] World Health Organization report, quoted by the American Institute of Health; and WebMD: The Effects of Stress on Your Body.

[2] Lorraine L. Janeczko, "Smartphones Allow Do-it-yourself Stress Hormone Tests," *Reuters*, July 4, 2014.

[3] Children's developing brain architecture is highly susceptible to early exposure to toxic stress. In the absence of protective factors, children's brains may respond by becoming more sensitized to stress and essentially hardwired to react much more strongly than someone else who didn't experience a lot of turmoil. Childhood stress can impact learning, memory and emotions, and behavior, health and employment prospects later in life. See Center on the Developing Child at Harvard University: www.developingchild.harvard.edu.

What besieges us so? The common themes emerging from polls and surveys should come as no surprise: health, jobs, finances, relationships, parenting and an ever-present sense of overwhelm regularly top the lists. A July 2014 poll by the Harvard School of Public Health, the Robert Wood Johnson Foundation and NPR found that almost half the public had experienced a major stress in the past year. Of those, nearly half were related to health. Others reported that too many overall responsibilities and financial problems were major contributors to their stress. Also in the highest-stressed categories: people living with chronic illness and disabilities, those with annual incomes under $20,000, people facing potentially dangerous situations in their jobs, single parents and parents of teens.

In the face of all this, is it possible to craft a meaningful set of rules to address stressful situations as diverse as job loss, health crises and disobedient teenagers on the one hand, and political discord, global warming and even war on the other? I spent those first years in the trenches writing doggedly about stress from every angle: I filed columns about relationship stress, work stress, job hunting stress, traffic stress, back-to-school stress, recession stress, stress among children, stress among the elderly . . . I wrote about lawyers gone Zen and meditating tech titans, athletes and bestselling authors. In column after column, I provided a laundry list of tips to help people through difficult circumstances.

Nearly everyone who discovered what I did for a living asked me some variation of the same question: *How can I manage all this stress in my life?* It was a veritable feast of distress and, at least according to a couple of surveys, I was a top influencer on the subject.

At some point my work began to take on a certain hamster-in-the-hamster-wheel feeling. With each new survey, study and product, the picture of stress grew more dismal and its impact more overwhelming.

The sense that things were not adding up began as a background whisper late in Year One and grew into a full roar as the next year wore on. Given how much I had hated being a lawyer, help came from the unlikeliest place: my legal training. In the first year of law school, students are assigned to read cases, dozens and dozens of them. When enough cases are read about a particular area of the law, patterns emerge. Eventually those patterns fit together to form an even larger context and meaning. This process is called "synthesis," and, as you might imagine, most law students become quite adept at synthesizing cases. It becomes second nature.

I had started my assignment with the baseline assumptions shared by most of us: Stress is pervasive. It is damaging. It can disable and even kill. We must find ways to avoid and minimize the stress in our lives.

These were not unreasonable assumptions, given the vast amount of research that points to the adverse impacts of stress.

But there was more—so much more—missing from the larger conversation about this health crisis: critical context that came not just from science but also philosophy, history, religion and other disciplines. Once these new pieces entered the equation, the picture of stress—our current cultural narrative of stress—began to change and a new picture began to emerge, as yet hazy and uncertain, but something important nonetheless.

Then, one day, more than a year after I had begun my journey into the stress vortex, the pieces finally took shape for me. There, suddenly, it stood: the reality of stress.

And it was not at all what I had imagined it to be.

The Elephant in the Room

There are many variations of the tale of the wise men and the elephant. The version I heard as a child in Iran, "An Elephant in the Dark," is by the Sufi mystic and poet Rumi:

> Some Hindus have an elephant to show.
> No one here has ever seen an elephant.
> They bring it at night to a dark room.
> One by one, we go in the dark and come out
> saying how we experience the animal.
> One of us happens to touch the trunk.
> "A water-pipe kind of creature."
> Another, the ear. "A very strong, always moving
> back and forth, fan-animal."
> Another, the leg. "I find it still,
> like a column on a temple."
> Another touches the curved back.
> "A leathery throne."
> Another, the cleverest, feels the tusk.
> "A rounded sword made of porcelain."
> He's proud of his description.
> Each of us touches one place
> and understands the whole that way.
> The palm and the fingers feeling in the dark are
> how the senses explore the reality of the elephant.
> If each of us held a candle there,
> and if we went in together,
> we could see it.

For many of us, stress has become that unknown elephant in a dark room. We do our best to feel around in the dark, to understand the whole by fumbling at pieces. Ultimately it is ever present—too close for comfort and too big to ignore. And yet a sense of the beast in its entirety eludes us.

This is why most of us cannot find lasting relief from stress. This is probably why you have picked up this book. Why it may not be your first (or fifth, or tenth) attempt to address the constant sense of overwhelm in your life. Why you may well have a nightstand/bookshelf/cupboard/desk/computer/smartphone overflowing with books/articles/apps promising relief. And why you are here, at this pass, yet again.

You are not alone.

Since 2007 the American Psychological Association has conducted an annual survey called "Stress in America." As you might imagine, the survey findings do not bode well for us. The 2013 survey reported "a scenario in which Americans consistently experience stress at levels higher than what they think is healthy."[4]

We are constantly exhorted to "avoid all stress." We do our best to follow this advice—so much so that stress and ways to relieve it have become big business. Entire industries have sprung up, simultaneously promising greater happiness and less stress.

The books, apps, gadgets and gizmos intended to help with stress relief and, more generally, happiness could fill a small warehouse. At last check, Amazon had more than thirty thousand books on the subjects. There are books by scientists, books by spiritualists, self-help books, stress reduction workbooks for women and for children; there are tomes on decluttering, mindfulness and yoga, books on stress physiology and stress manage-

---

[4] "Stress in America: Missing the Health Care Connection," American Psychological Association, 2013.

ment for dummies, not to mention memoirs devoted to stress relief and its first cousin, happiness.

Billions of dollars, millions of Google search results, dozens of bestsellers and self-styled gurus later, and yet the stress-free lives we long for continue to elude us. All indications are that the advice to "avoid stress" is a futile strategy when it comes to the runaway anxieties of our modern lives.[5] Which only makes us doubly stressed: We are now also stressed about being stressed!

"Is 'Stressed Out' the New Normal?" asked the American Psychological Association in 2013.

Why?

Why exactly is stress so bad *now*? Didn't our ancestors have to outrun a mountain lion or two on their way back from fetching dinner? Didn't they have to survive plagues, floods, famines and depressions? Fight world wars? Compared with our hardy forebears, we live in relative ease. How did we end up with this modern burden of living in one of the most trying times in the history of humankind? What changed?

---

[5] All mentions of "anxiety" in this book refer to its general meaning as "a feeling of worry, nervousness and unease," and not to its clinical definition as a nervous disorder.

CHAPTER TWO

The Most Trying Times

In his 1948 Pulitzer Prize–winning poem *The Age of Anxiety*, W. H. Auden sought to examine humanity's quest to find its way in a modern, fast-changing and increasingly industrialized world. Auden wrote:

> We would rather be ruined than changed
> We would rather die in our dread
> Than climb the cross of the moment
> And let our illusions die.

The Age of Anxiety, observes journalist and author Daniel Smith, came to "characterize the consciousness of our era, the awareness of everything perilous about the modern world: the degradation of the environment, nuclear energy, religious fundamentalism, threats to privacy and the family, drugs, pornography, violence, terrorism . . . As a sticker on the bumper of the Western world, 'the age of anxiety' has been ubiquitous for more than six decades now."[6]

"We see ourselves as living in more stressful times," James Gross, one of the world's top experts on emotions and emotion regulation, once told me in an interview. "But it is also true that in many historical periods people seemed to think they were in the most stressful times ever."

I had been busy typing notes as he spoke, but this stopped me cold.

"What are you saying?" I asked.

"It's actually a very common experience to see yourself as living in a particularly stressful period," he continued. "I'm questioning the premise that we are living in necessarily more stressful times."

It was the first time I had questioned the assumption that we are living in "the most stressful times." This notion of stresses and stressors, of feeling constantly overwhelmed, has become so commonplace in our society that the terrible anxiety of our times and the havoc it wreaks on our mental and physical health is a given, widely accepted as near dogma. Yes, things seem bad— and, at times, awful. But if it is true that our circumstances are not, taken on the whole, better or worse than our predecessors', then why the stress epidemic? Did we just get better at identifying and diagnosing?

Leaving aside the unanswerable question of just who had it worse—us or our ancestors—let us consider for a moment what is an irrefutable fact of our times, and unprecedented in the history of humankind: that we are now much more aware of events, both global and hyperlocal, than ever before.

---

[6] Daniel Smith, "It's Still the Age of Anxiety. Or Is It?," *New York Times*, January 14, 2012.

We have unparalleled access, in real time and conveyed through image and sound, to polarizing and upsetting events near and far, streamed to us through media on a slew of devices, including one most of us carry on our bodies constantly, as if it were an appendage. Our nervous systems, built to seek out information all around us in an adaptive way, have a field day with this level of access. By knowing about threats, we reason, we may be able to prevent them from happening to us, so we seek out bad news, effectively bombarding ourselves virtually around the clock with negative information.[7]

So while in this era we must deal with our own specific set of stressors both big and small—traffic gridlock, constantly buzzing devices and multitasking in the best of scenarios; economic meltdowns, global warming and terrorism in the worst—our brains process these stresses in the same way as our ancestors' brains did when they faced dire life-or-death circumstances. The difference is, we endure them constantly.

Echoes from the Past

Continual access means that we are exposed to more potential stressors throughout the day, but access alone does not solve the puzzle of why, within one century, our leading causes of death shifted from tuberculosis, pneumonia and influenza to a range of maladies that can be caused or made worse by stress: heart disease, cancer, adult-onset diabetes and Alzheimer's.[8] An important clue to this question lies in the era of *Mad Men*, with an

---

[7] Professor James Gross, Stanford University.

[8] Robert M. Sapolsky, "How to Relieve Stress," Berkeley Greater Good Science Center, March 22, 2012.

unlikely set of malefactors and their nefarious agenda. Yes, this book has a villain and that villain is not stress.

While the stress response itself is as old as life, our concept of stress is reasonably modern. It hails back to a group of hapless rats in a 1950s science lab and a researcher named Hans Hugo Bruno Selye.[9] Selye was an Austrian-born physician and biochemist. He attended university in Prague, but was forced to flee the Nazis in the early 1930s. He found his way to Canada, where he accepted work in the endocrinology department at the University of Montréal. As the junior member of his team, Selye was tasked with the unenviable chore of venturing out to a slaughterhouse each day and returning with a bucket of freshly harvested cow ovaries. The scientists in the lab would then process the organs into an extract and inject them into female lab rats. They were looking for evidence of a new female hormone.

Over the course of the many autopsies that ensued, Selye failed to find any such evidence, but he did observe something else rather interesting. The injected rats suffered from a "curious triad of symptoms: peptic ulcers in the stomach and upper intestine, enlarged adrenal glands and shrunken immune tissues."[10]

To determine whether these symptoms were related to the specific substance being injected or not, Selye began injecting the animals with extracts made from other organs. The same trio of symptoms appeared once again. Emboldened, Selye expanded his inquiry further, to see whether the symptoms would also result from other trauma. And so he began inflicting a variety of stressors on the rats and examining their responses.

---

[9] Except as noted, this section about the history of stress is drawn from my 2012 interview with Harvard science historian Anne Harrington and her stunning history of mind-body medicine, *The Cure Within*.

[10] Harrington, *The Cure Within*.

"[N]o matter what type of damage I inflicted on an experimental animal, if it survived long enough and the stressor was sufficiently strong, the typical combination would be produced: adrenal hyperactivity, lymphatic atrophy and peptic ulcers," wrote Selye in his 1979 memoir, *The Stress of My Life.*

Years later Selye would recall how as a young medical student in Prague he had observed patients with different diseases presenting a common set of symptoms—feeling weak and listless, having similar facial expressions—which he identified generally as "the syndrome of just being sick." He suspected then that the symptoms were connected somehow. He wrote: "I asked myself . . . why so many people suffer from heart disease, high blood pressure, arthritis, or mental disturbances. These are not completely stereotyped signs of all illness, yet they are so frequent that I could not help suspecting some nonspecific common factor in their causation."[11]

Selye formalized this nonspecific common factor in a word he borrowed from metallurgy. That word was "stress."

In a conceptually groundbreaking paper published in *Nature* in 1936, Selye observed that stress "as a whole seems to represent a generalised effort of the organism to adapt itself to new conditions." It was, therefore, a "general adaptation syndrome" that unfolded in three stages. During the first stage, the "alarm phase," the animal perceived a threat and underwent the physiological changes needed to either fight or take flight. (The fight-or-flight response had already been described by scientist Walter Bradford Cannon in the 1920s.)[12]

Next came the "stage of resistance," where the animal's

---

[11] Hans Selye, quoted in Harrington, *The Cure Within.*

[12] Hans Selye, *The Stress of Life,* quoted in Mark Jackson, *The Age of Stress, Science and the Search for Stability.*

body effectively adapted to the threat, reversing the physiological changes it had gone through during the previous phase and reverting back to normal.

But if the threat continued beyond the animal's capacity to handle, a third phase—a "stage of exhaustion"—would trigger symptoms very much like those that had manifested during the alarm phase. It was here, in the exhaustion stage, that adaptation would fail and the body wear down, thus opening the door for disease and even death.

The key, Selye wrote, was adaptation: "The secret of health and happiness lies in successful adjustment to the ever changing conditions on this globe; the penalties for failure in this great process of adaptation are disease and unhappiness."[13]

Selye was incredibly proud of his new discovery, deeming it "my child [who] will outlive me."[14] He even took great pride in recounting how some of his earlier theories about the "syndrome of just being sick" had been met with scorn by his professors. Years later, he would feel vindicated: "Stress will have been my cathedral. I shall polish and perfect it."

According to historian Anne Harrington, Selye faced serious doubts among his fellow scientists early on. Many of Selye's colleagues, including Cannon, were skeptical about his theories: "They suggested that Selye had exaggerated the uniformity of the response seen in different experimental situations, had not adequately defined stress as a concept, and that in any event, many of his experiments were highly artificial and had little if anything to say about pathophysiological processes seen in a clinical context."[15]

---

[13] Ibid.

[14] Selye, *The Stress of My Life*; "The Secret History Behind the Science of Stress," NPR, July 7, 2014.

[15] Harrington, *The Cure Within*.

Selye would not be ignored. He stopped trying to convince skeptical scientists and began instead to look beyond his peers for support. His ambitious campaign involved cultivating an extended audience that included military psychiatrists. Selye also appealed to popular magazines and their broad base of readers.

Very soon Hans Selye would also catch the eye of another group: the tobacco industry. And that particular coupling would profoundly impact our culture and the way we experience stress today.

The Rise of the Culture of Stress

At the turn of the twentieth century cardiovascular disease was relatively rare, responsible for fewer than 10 percent of deaths worldwide. By mid-century, however, coronary heart disease had skyrocketed, particularly in the American and European populations, now suddenly representing the single greatest cause of death. A number of epidemiological efforts were launched to determine the cause of the disease's sudden rise. Among these, the Framingham Heart Study was the first to confirm a clear link between smoking and heart disease.

As researchers began to cast a wary eye at cigarettes, the tobacco industry was caught in a dilemma. With lawsuits nipping at Big Tobacco's heels, tobacco companies began doing what vulnerable corporations trying to protect billions in profits have done before and since: attempt to lay blame elsewhere.

Two San Francisco cardiologists, Ray Rosenman and Meyer Friedman, formed an alternate theory about the high incidence of heart disease based on their observation that the front edges of their waiting room chairs were worn down by fidgeting, impatient patients, many of whom happened to be white-collar managers. Could it be, the doctors mused, that it was personality traits shared by those who held particular jobs that put them at risk for heart attacks?

To validate their theory, Rosenman and Friedman surveyed several hundred San Francisco businessmen and general practitioners. From a list of personality characteristics, an overwhelming majority of respondents selected the characteristic of having "excessive competitive drive and meeting deadlines." The doctors ran with this, coining the clever moniker that would become embedded in our lexicon to describe the competitive and the deadline-driven: The type A personality had entered the room.

By this time, Selye's relentless efforts had paid off. His theories had "permeated medical thinking and influenced medical research in every land, probably more rapidly and more intensely than any other theory of disease ever proposed."[16] Selye traveled the world preaching the gospel of stress, and when all was said and done, his academic oeuvre would include more than fifteen hundred books and articles.[17]

Selye, Rosenman and Friedman all had one thing in common: they were among the scores of scientists being groomed—and funded—by Big Tobacco.

Dr. Mark Petticrew is the director of public health research at the London School of Hygiene and Tropical Medicine. "Not obvious" is how he describes his background—he earned a PhD in psychology, but throughout his career he was always interested in stress and heart disease, which besieged a large percentage of the population in his native Northern Ireland.

[16] F. L. Engel, quoted in Harrington, The Cure Within.

[17] "The Secret History Behind the Science of Stress," NPR.

In 1985, when Petticrew was a young researcher at Queen's University in Belfast, he attended a lecture by an American cardiologist who was on a speaking tour in the United Kingdom. "The lecture was basically a side shot of the whole stress discussion," Petticrew explains. "I was in the first year of my PhD and fairly green. And the thing that really struck me was that his trip was sponsored by the UK Milk Marketing Board. I remember wondering why the dairy industry would be funding an American stress researcher. I was studying a lot about stress and heart disease, and up until that moment I hadn't come across the idea that some of these areas of scientific interest were also being used and adopted by industries trying to protect themselves." The speaker that day was Ray Rosenman. Petticrew had no way of knowing it then, but in two decades their paths would again intersect.

In the late 1990s, as part of a legal settlement, tobacco companies were required to release millions of top secret documents. Many were archived online. The documents represented a treasure trove of memoranda exposing much of the tobacco industry's strategies and tactics, including their efforts to recruit scientists and academics to protect the industry's interests. In 2005, Petticrew and his colleagues in London began sifting through the documents. What they discovered calls into question our entire cultural narrative about stress.

By all indications, contact between Selye and Big Tobacco began in 1958 when he wrote to the American Tobacco Company seeking funding. His request was denied, but the following year an attorney defending the company in a lawsuit wrote to Selye for help with the legal defense. That attorney, Edwin Jacob, wanted to argue that a statistical association between smoking and cancer was not proof that one caused the other. He offered Selye a thousand dollars for his cooperation on the case. Selye agreed and supplied Jacob with a memorandum, but he declined to testify and asked not to be quoted.

In one 1966 exchange among tobacco industry lawyers, William Shinn, representing Philip Morris and others, observed that Selye's earlier memorandum had been problematic because "the approach appeared to be one that conceded some carcinogenic factor in tobacco." He also reported that Selye was willing to write a paper on smoking and stress, but wanted guidance on what to write. "Dr. Selye should comment on the unlikelihood of there being a mechanism by which smoking could cause cardiovascular disease," he wrote. The tobacco lawyer also thought Selye ought to emphasize the "stressful" effects of antismoking messages on the American population.[18]

Selye would meet with the industry lawyers again the following year to advise on a defense of smoking as "prophylactic and curative."

Together, Shinn and Selye concocted a theory they would sell to the public. They argued for the "desirability of adjusting to a stressful life by seeking diversions." What types of diversions? Smoking, naturally. "This reference to 'diversions' reflected Selye's view that disease was a result of unsuccessful adaption to environmental stimuli. This stress could be counteracted by other stimuli, a process he called 'deviation,' of which smoking was a form," observed Petticrew and his colleagues.

Shinn and Selye also had a dissemination strategy: "The theory should be promulgated through articles, books, TV appearances etc. . . . with the creation of [the] image of smoking as a right for many people—as a natural act for man."[19]

---

[18] M. P. Petticrew and K. Lee, "The 'Father of Stress' Meets 'Big Tobacco': Hans Selye and the Tobacco Industry," *American Journal of Public Health*, March 2011.

[19] Petticrew and Lee, "The 'Father of Stress' Meets 'Big Tobacco.'"

Selye would go on to argue against government overregulation of science and public health, antismoking legislation, advertising restrictions, health warnings and restrictions on tar and nicotine. "The question is not 'to smoke or not to smoke,'" he once testified, "but to smoke or drink, eat, drive a car—or simply fret. Since we cannot discard our surplus energy, we must occupy it somehow . . . Often more damage is done by creating, through well-meant crusades of enlightenment, innumerable hypochondriacs whose main sickness is really the fear of sickness." The problem, apparently, was not smoking, but the antismoking campaigns!

Hans Selye, who never publicly disclosed his alliance with the tobacco industry, was rewarded handsomely.

Harrington observes that by the 1970s, the narrative of stress as the plight of a modern people whose lives were so full of stimuli and stressors that their bodies were prone to disease had effectively taken hold. Discussions of stress abounded in magazines, self-help literature, advice columns and elsewhere. "In 1981 the Institute of Medicine estimated that some $35 million had been spent on stress research in 1979 alone," writes Harrington. The Institute also made note of a thriving industry of stress relief remedies and literature, and many stress-related legal cases and workplace health disputes.[20]

By then Hans Selye's theories were firmly rooted in American culture. His narrative of stress—and the tobacco companies'—had become ours. Headline after headline sounded the same devastating alarm: "Stress May Be the Worst Killer of Modern Era." "Modern Life Includes Toll Exacted in Terms of Stress." "Stress: Modern Man's Silent Enemy." "Premature Aging the Result of Modern Stress."[21] And on and on, up to the present day.

---

[20] Harrington, *The Cure Within.*

[21] Sampling of magazine headlines, quoted in Harrington, *The Cure Within.*

If the scientific integrity of all that foundational research on stress is questionable, what does that mean for our concept of stress today and the narratives of stress that permeate our society?

"We should, at the very least, be acknowledging the ways in which the tobacco industry has muddied the waters here," says Petticrew.

CHAPTER THREE

The Power of Perception

Learning how to think really means learning how to exercise some control over how and what you think. It means being conscious and aware enough to choose what you pay attention to and to choose how you construct meaning from experience.

—DAVID FOSTER WALLACE

" I want to start with a game," says neuroscientist and artist Beau Lotto at the outset of an experiment he conducts with his audience. "To win this game, all you have to do is see the reality that's in front of you as it really is."

Lotto's first game involves two panels of colored dots—one series against a white background, the other against a black background. One dot in the first panel, he tells us, is the same color as a dot in the second. Can you figure out which one?

Most of us cannot.

Next, he shows a black-and-white image of a jungle scene.

"Can any of you see the predator that's about to jump out at you."

Again, we cannot.

"If you haven't seen it yet, you're dead," he says. We chuckle nervously. He modifies the image slightly and there, suddenly, stands our predator, prepared to pounce.

Lotto uses these games to show that even our most fundamental perceptions are subject to interpretation. Seeing reality is not as easy as we might think, even when it comes to simple shapes and colors.

The variable is context. "The world around us is physics devoid of meaning, whereas our perception of the world is meaning devoid of physics," says Lotto.

Human perception begins when the brain receives data from the body's five senses. The mind then processes and applies meaning to the sensory information. The rub is that sensory information can mean just about anything. It's what we do with that information that matters. The exact same image can have an infinite number of sources in the real world. And so when it comes to perception—seeing, feeling, hearing, sensing things—there is no such thing as objectivity.

Humans evolved to make sense of things. Every time a stimulus comes to us, our brain does the efficient thing: It responds based on past experience. In so doing, the brain continuously redefines normality. It is being shaped, literally, as a consequence of trial and error.

"The brain did not evolve to see the world the way it really is—we can't," says Lotto. "We can't help but see things according to history—our own history and that of our ancestors—because we are defined by ecology. Not by our biology, not by our DNA, but by our history of interactions." Our experiences are less the result of reality than they are the fruits of our historical and social contexts.

Consider, as an example, two different scenarios.

In the first, it is a key game on the road to the NCAA tournament. The crowd is roaring, electrified. The players run up and down the court. It's the final ten seconds of the final game and the teams are tied. A player, a young African-American man, steals the ball and hustles down the court. The crowd goes crazy. He runs, almost soars, sweat glistening on his brown arms and face. Five seconds left. He shoots. He scores. All hell breaks loose. The adoring fans go wild, chanting the player's name in a rousing celebration.

Now imagine a second scene: It is a mild evening in late February. An African-American teenager leaves a house he is visiting to walk to a nearby 7-Eleven, where he buys a bag of Skittles and a drink. On his way back, he catches the attention of a neighborhood watch captain driving around in his car. The older man calls the police and reports a black male wearing a hoodie sweatshirt who looks "real suspicious." The 911 operator tells the watch captain that police officers have been dispatched and instructs him to cease his pursuit of the boy.

But the man pursues anyway. At some point, he stops his car and confronts the teenager with a handgun. There is yelling, a physical altercation and then a gunshot. By the time the police arrive, the boy is lying face down in the grass, mortally wounded. The neighborhood watch captain says he acted in self-defense against a teen with nothing in his hands but a bag of candy and a can of iced tea.[22]

This second story, of course, is that of the real-life encounter between Trayvon Martin and George Zimmerman, a tragedy built upon context and perceptions. Consider the different ways

---

[22] Charles M. Blow, "The Curious Case of Trayvon Martin," *New York Times*, March 17, 2012.

many Americans see the agency of black men. In certain contexts, like on a basketball court during March Madness, we are perfectly comfortable celebrating black males. But take those exact bodies and place them in a different context—walking down the street in a predominantly white neighborhood—and that perception of black masculinity quickly changes context. And now our stories about that black male may suddenly create a life-or-death scenario.[23]

Our stories get inside our heads and habits. They affect our perception. They shape everything—our taste in food, our sensibilities, what we think is good, bad or evil. Virtually nothing occurs in isolation. This profound social influence is known as "habitus." It is acquired through activities and experiences of everyday life, and is often taken for granted. Relying unconsciously on the stories that have been handed down to us serves us well.

Until it doesn't.

There is a sort of intuitive logic to the idea of stress and its harms that overrides the origins of our current story lines. But ignoring where and how these stories came from, and being blind to their impact, would be an enormous mistake. Our stories are vital because they shape our reality. "People are trapped in history and history is trapped in them," wrote James Baldwin. This is particularly true about our perceptions of adversity.

"Between stimulus and response there is a space. In that space is our power to choose our response. In our response lies our growth and our freedom," wrote psychiatrist Viktor Frankl, who survived many years in several of the most notorious Nazi concentration camps.

Our stories provide the context in which our perceptions form. They serve as the connective tissue between stimulus—what

---

[23] Professor Ruha Benjamin, Princeton University.

happens to us from day to day—and our response. As such, exploring that space is vital to our physical and emotional well-being. Because therein lies our future.

Sometimes we find ourselves at a crossroads, in a place of uncertainty, faced with stories and perceptions born of falsehood, misunderstanding and bias. Echoing Frankl, Beau Lotto says of those types of perceptions: "We are responding and not choosing."

Did we choose most of our prevailing stories about stress? We did not. They were crafted for us, behind the scenes, by malefactors with a Machiavellian agenda. What's more, many of these false narratives stand in stark contrast to centuries of wisdom and spiritual insight about the profound power of adversity: "The wound is where the light enters you," wrote the poet Rumi.

Another poet, Khalil Gibran, observed:

> Your joy is your sorrow unmasked . . .
> The deeper that sorrow carves into your being,
>   the more joy you can contain.

We need a new cultural narrative about stress. We need it desperately and immediately. We are attempting to navigate new worlds with distorted maps, conquer new territories with false scripts. It is time for us to take our story back and bring it in line with the untainted realities that are presented to us by our scientists, historians, philosophers, spiritual guides and others.

Beau Lotto says that the underlying goal of his research is to help people transform by enabling them to understand and become part of learning about their own perceptions. He hopes people will walk away from his experiments not with an understanding of color, but with a better understanding of themselves.

The first step, he says, is through self-awareness: a greater consciousness of our stories, how they came to us, how they weave through our everyday and how they help shape our world.

We must become aware of the connection between the present and the past. We may have a story of stress that does not serve us, but we have the power to choose our perceptions, to choose different stories, more aligned with reality, that do serve us better. We can choose a narrative that helps reframe the stressors that besiege and overwhelm us as catalysts that become our strengths and guides.

We can choose better.

CHAPTER FOUR

The Physiology of Stress

Let's take a few minutes to separate fact from myth when it comes to stress and our bodies. The stress response is a particularly brilliant aspect of our design. It heightens efficiency and mobilizes strength and energy at the exact moment when our bodies need it most: when we sense threats in our immediate surroundings.[24]

The chain of events in the stress cycle begins with the body in balance. The body perceives a threat. It rises to the challenge and transforms to handle the stressor. The crisis is handled. The body returns to balance.

Doesn't this sound like a familiar tale? How about any num-

---

[24] This chapter relies on and weaves together numerous interviews with Dr. Rajita Sinha, director of the Yale Stress Center; "Understanding the Stress Response," *Harvard Mental Health Letter*, March 2011; writing by Robert Sapolsky and other authorities listed in Selected Sources.

ber of our superhero stories? The stress response is, in many ways, no less than a superpower.

Imagine one of our ancestors—let's call him Aleph—making his way through the woods on a warm afternoon. He looks down at the small, lifeless beast he's clutching and feels a thrill about the catch. He and his kin will not go hungry this evening. Suddenly Aleph senses a vague movement to his right. It comes from a shadowy patch just beyond the trees. He can't make out anything. He focuses his eyes and trains his ears in the direction of the sound. Then a second rustle, closer this time. His heart jumps as he discerns the shape: sleek, impossibly large, with eyes narrowed and body poised in his direction. Electricity shoots through him. One of two things may happen: Aleph prepares to fight, or he drops his catch and runs faster than he thought possible.

Let's assume that Aleph is able to escape and return safely to his abode so he can help walk us through our hypothetical stress cycle: Balance. Rev up. Shift down. Return to balance.

Balance

Our bodies—every cell, organ and system—need a degree of internal balance to operate optimally. This balance, known as homeostasis, requires that a symphony of bodily functions keeps our internal environment within a narrow range. The star players in this symphony are optimal blood sugar levels and ideal body temperature. Since it's impossible for anyone to live in a state free of stimuli, our bodies are constantly thrown off balance in countless different ways, both big and small and good and bad, every single day: exercise, angry exchanges in traffic, illness, injury, a fraught relationship with the boss, the anticipation of a first kiss.

In the broadest sense, a stressor is *any* kind of stimulus that knocks a person out of balance. That stimulus can be real or it can be imagined. Consider the word "imagined"—because it is generally agreed that the devil of modern stress often lies within the particulars of how things are perceived. That is, stress is not *what* happens to you, but *how* you react.

Let's return to our ancestor, Aleph. It is a day or two later and he's wandering in the woods again. Once again Aleph sees and hears something, possibly a threat. His sense organs—eyes and ears in particular—send information to the amygdala. A small almond-shaped mass, the amygdala helps process emotions and, in particular, the fear response. Aleph's amygdala interprets the incoming sights and sounds. It determines that there is a threat and sends a distress signal to the hypothalamus.

Rev Up!

The hypothalamus, also about the size of an almond, acts as the control center. Once Aleph's hypothalamus receives the signal, it takes charge and directs a number of important functions. It communicates with the rest of the body through the autonomic nervous system, which regulates crucial automatic bodily functions that are critical to how Aleph responds to the threat he perceives. His breathing, heartbeat, blood pressure, digestive processes, dilation or constriction of key blood vessels and small airways in the lung—all are impacted.

Aleph's sympathetic nervous system steps up, mobilizing resources to give him an immediate burst of energy. His adrenal glands have been alerted by the hypothalamus too. They secrete hormones—in particular, epinephrine, also known as adrenaline—into his bloodstream. The epinephrine surge triggers important physiological changes to Aleph's heart rate and pulse, his muscle strength, his blood pressure, his sugar metabolism. Now Aleph begins to breathe fast. The airways in his lungs open, letting him extract as much oxygen as possible from every breath he takes. That extra oxygen goes straight to his brain. Aleph finds himself more alert, his thinking is crystal clear, his senses are sharp.

Blood sugar and fat are released from storage sites throughout Aleph's body. They flood his bloodstream, delivering even more energy. His nonessential systems—his digestion, his sex drive, among others—shut down to provide him with even more energy to deal with the emergency. Aleph's immune defenses are enhanced.

Minutes later, even as the adrenaline rush begins to subside, a second component of Aleph's stress response system kicks in. Now the command center has activated interactions among the hypothalamus, the pituitary gland and the adrenal glands to keep the sympathetic nervous system revved up. If Aleph's brain continues to perceive danger, a relay race of hormones makes its way to the adrenal glands, prompting them to release the big guns: Enter cortisol.

Shift Down and Return to Balance

Once the threat, either real or perceived, has passed and the inflammatory processes—those that were triggered in Aleph's body to help him rise to the occasion—have done their work, the second part of Aleph's autonomic nervous system, the parasympathetic nervous system, kicks in. It acts like a brake, promoting the "rest and digest" response to calm the body.

Cortisol's job now is to regulate the inflammatory response and to restore homeostasis: balance. Cortisol influences many of the changes in Aleph's body that helped him respond to the stress of his encounter. When its work is done, cortisol levels fall. Aleph is back in balance.

Where Does Our Superpower Go Wrong?

One of my favorite observations about the dilemma of modern stress was made by Robert Sapolsky, the brilliant Stanford neuroendocrinologist whose decades of research have taught us much of what we know about chronic stress. Sapolsky writes:

> For 99 percent of the species on this planet, stress is three minutes of screaming terror in the savannah, after which either it's over with or you're over with. That's all you need to know about the subject if you're a zebra or a lion. If you're a human, though, you've got to expand the definition of a stressor in a very critical way. If you're running from a lion, your blood pressure is 180 over 120. But you're not suffering from high blood pressure—you're saving your life. Have this same thing happen when you're stuck in traffic, and you're not saving your life. Instead you are suffering from stress-induced hypertension.[25]

The most important thing you need to know about toxic stress is that it involves 1) strong, 2) unrelieved activation of the body's stress management system, in 3) the absence of protective factors.

Hormones released during the fight-or-flight response—the same ones that helped our ancestors flee danger—have a devas-

----

[25] Sapolsky, "How to Relieve Stress."

tating effect when they are sustained over long periods of time. Minutes or hours of stress are stabilized by cortisol (and other hormones). But chronic stress—the kind that lasts days, weeks, months and even years—is when we begin to wade toward the murky waters of disease.

Normally cortisol levels are high in the morning and drop throughout the course of the day. But among people who suffer from chronic stress, cortisol levels remain high throughout the day, with less of a decrease in the evening. Chronic exposure to cortisol causes physiological changes that make it increasingly difficult to shut down the stress response. Over a prolonged period of stress, body tissue becomes desensitized to cortisol and the hormone loses its effectiveness in regulating inflammation. This constant state of inflammation turns the stress response into a runaway train, which leaves in its wake a world of physiological wreckage.

Once the body has lost its ability to regulate the inflammatory response and reestablish balance, chronic inflammation creates the ideal breeding ground for the development and progression of illness, including depression, heart disease, rheumatoid arthritis, diabetes and, yes, even cancer.[26] That's when that same inflammatory response that allowed Aleph to outrun the tiger and heal from his wounds becomes deadly.

Cementing this damage is our stories about stress—stories that, in turn, create the context for our perception of everyday stressors. It's what Stanford researcher Alia Crum and her colleagues call the "stress mindset," which is essentially our current cultural narrative that we are overtaxed, overburdened and overwhelmed, and that all that stress is making us sick and possibly

---

[26] See Sheldon Cohen, Denise Janicki-Deverts, William J. Doyle, Gregory E. Miller, Ellen Frank, Bruce S. Rabin and Ronald B. Turner, "Chronic Stress, Glucocorticoid Receptor Resistance, Inflammation, and Disease Risk," *Proceedings of the National Academy of Sciences*, April 2012.

killing us.[27] You have heard of the placebo effect. The stress mindset operates as a sort of "nocebo effect," in which negative expectations do us harm.

In fact, stress as an all-consuming burden represents only a part of the picture, though most of us live as if it's the entire story, the beginning and the end, the point of departure and the destination. The mantra *I am stressed* plays out in our lives in an endless, self-defeating loop. Our stories of stress leach into our lives, stunt our growth, dull our joy. They affect us, body and soul.

Stress can kill, yes, but a growing body of research corroborates the age-old wisdom that stress can also enhance and strengthen.[28] There is much nuance lost in the current conversation about stress, which is exactly why it is urgent that we arm ourselves by becoming conscious of our assumptions about stress and understand what stress really is—and what it isn't.

The Stress Spectrum: Good, Bad, Tolerable

Stanford neuroimmunologist Firdaus Dhabhar's pioneering research helps us to better understand the stress spectrum, with chronic stress at one end, acute stress at the other and tolerable stress forming the shades of gray in between. His experiments highlight a range of benefits associated with the acute stress response, revealing that short spurts of stress can enhance the immune response so that we recover better and faster from both psychological threats and physical ones.

---

[27] Alia J. Crum, Peter Salovey and Shawn Achor, "Rethinking Stress: The Role of Mindsets in Determining the Stress Response," *Journal of Personality and Social Psychology*, April 2013. Also see Heidi Grant Halvorson, "How You Can Benefit from All Your Stress," *Harvard Business Review*, March 14, 2013.

[28] Ibid.

Dhabhar began his journey as something of a contrarian. He was a young researcher, struck by what was at the time "an overwhelming dogma that all stress is bad" because it depresses the immune system. The view is based partly on the fact that during periods of acute stress, blood levels of T cells—a type of white blood cell of critical importance to immunity—plummets.

But something about this did not add up for Dhabhar. He wondered why the immune system of a person preparing to fight or flee would be shutting down—rather than ramping up—in response to that threat. "From a fundamental biological perspective, the main reason all organisms were given the ability to mount the stress response was to enable survival. So it was strange to me that stress would always or necessarily be bad," he says.

Dhabhar formed a theory: What if, at the perception of a threat, those immune cells that were leaving the blood were traveling instead to more strategic sites? Studying rats exposed to short-term stressors, the researcher and his colleagues found that, under resting conditions, immune cells remained in organs like the spleen. But the moment a stressor was introduced, those immune cells surged into the bloodstream, then quickly exited to take positions in key sites throughout the body.[29]

Dhabhar showed that patients who mount a robust short-term stress response during surgery recover better than patients who don't mount a similar response. He also found that introducing a stressor (like a short bout of exercise) prior to vaccinations significantly enhances the impact of the vaccine.

Other stress researchers are extending our understanding of good stress: They have shown that short bursts of stress can boost brain plasticity, and enhance memory and learning. Weill

---

[29] TED Talent Search, "Firdaus Dhabhar: The Positive Effects of Stress," YouTube video, June 25, 2012. https://www.youtube.com/watch?v=nsc83N-Q1q4.

Cornell professor Conor Liston found that periods of acute stress can translate into greater focus and alertness.[30]

Dhabhar is still asking some brilliant—and unconventional—questions. Might it be possible, for instance, to use the body's response to acute stress to enhance the immune systems of cancer patients? "We are not questioning the wealth of research emerging about toxic stress, but what we are asking is, why ignore this other part of the equation, especially when there may be tremendous benefits associated with harnessing it to our advantage?"

Tolerate, Adapt, Evolve

One of my children was a toddler and the other a preschooler when I found out I had cancer. My diagnosis was grave, and during the long months of uncertainty while I underwent surgery, chemo and radiation, my husband and I became concerned about how the fraught atmosphere and stress in our home was affecting our children. We knew that unrelenting childhood stress has the potential to overwhelm children in a tsunami of serious and lifelong health problems.

At the time, my daughter was attending Bing Nursery, the laboratory preschool at Stanford University, and it was from the world-renowned child psychologists at Bing that I first learned about the major protective factors that can downgrade toxic stress into what is considered "tolerable stress."

Tolerable stress shares many characteristics with toxic stress, and the line between the two is often blurred.[31] The former also

---

[30] Kristin Sainani, "What, Me Worry?" *Stanford Magazine*, May/June 2014.

[31] "Key Concepts: Toxic Stress," Center on the Developing Child at Harvard University: www.developingchild.harvard.edu.

tends to arise when we deal with longer-term difficulties, like losing a loved one, living through a natural disaster or suffering from a serious injury. Like toxic stress, tolerable stress is severe enough to be harmful, to disrupt brain architecture. But it is marked by "breaks, buffers and protective factors," interspersing those peaks of acute stress with valleys of low to no stress, the rest areas that Dhabhar refers to as "the green zones." It is these breaks and buffers that form the line of defense against the potential damage of chronic stress.

The Wreckage

A psychology professor is lecturing students about stress management. He raises a glass of water and asks: "How heavy is this glass?"

The students venture a number of guesses. Each time, the professor shrugs. When the students give up, he replies: "The weight of the glass doesn't matter. What matters is how long I've been holding it. It is light if held for a few minutes; more difficult if held for an hour; and impossible if held for an entire day."

The longer you hold it, the heavier it becomes.

The story, variations of which occasionally crop up on social media, is an interesting (if oversimplified) illustration of why chronic stress is so taxing. Triggered frequently enough and without adequate breaks, buffers and protective factors, stress becomes chronic. And at the point when stress is unrelenting and traumatic—*or when we perceive it to be unrelenting and traumatic*—the stress becomes toxic.

Most of us may no longer be facing life-or-death perils, but we *are* facing a variety of other difficult circumstances, like working endless shifts in demanding and thankless jobs that we are terrified of losing, or facing crushing debt, or trying to single-handedly raise children while working multiple jobs. The stress response is damaging when it becomes sustained, uncontrollable and overwhelming, such that people can't even conceive of options to solve their problems.[32]

Chronic stress takes a cumulative toll on both physical and mental health. The brain area most vulnerable to stress, including early childhood stress, is the prefrontal cortex, which is crucial for metabolic homeostasis, or stability, as well as for survival and adaptation. The prefrontal cortex is the region important for self-regulatory activities of all kinds, both emotional and cognitive, including impulse control and self-discipline, long-term planning, and regulation of emotion, cognition and desires.

Toxic stress shrinks the hippocampus, which is associated mainly with memory, particularly long-term memory. In the amygdala, which plays a key role in the processing of emotions including fear, the opposite happens. Stress expands the amygdala, rendering it "hyper-reactive, hysterical," which Robert Sapolsky observes helps to explain the connection between stress and anxiety disorders.[33]

Constant battering by stress—the toxic kind—wears down our ability to counteract potentially dangerous desires, such as cravings for addictive substances or foods. Control over impulsive and dangerous behavior may also wane. This is the dynamic that places children from troubled home environments and people suffering from addictions most at risk.

The damage here is to the mesolimbic dopamine system, which plays a key role in the neurobiology of addiction. Dopamine is a neurotransmitter that helps control the brain's reward and plea-

---

[32] This section is drawn primarily from my interviews with Dr. Rajita Sinha of the Yale Stress Center and from Dr. Robert Sapolsky's highly colorful description of the impacts of toxic stress in "How to Relieve Stress."

[33] Sapolsky, "How to Relieve Stress."

sure centers. Chronic stress depletes dopamine, reducing our ability to experience pleasure and making us more susceptible to depression.[34] The havoc extends to the cardiovascular system.

The prolonged activation of the stress response system is harmful to adults, but in children it is particularly damaging. It has the potential to disrupt development of brain architecture and other organs. It can also increase the risk for stress-related disease and cognitive impairment for life. "The more adverse experiences in childhood, the greater the likelihood of developmental delays and later health problems, including heart disease, diabetes, substance abuse and depression."[35] (However, research also points to a number of buffers that can prevent or reverse the damage of the toxic stress response in children. Key among these protective factors is supportive and responsive relationships with caring adults.[36])

In yet another interesting nuance, as damaging as life's most challenging circumstances may be to our health, the effects of chronic stress are not necessarily permanent. The human brain turns out to be extremely dynamic, offering potential for normalizing or regrowth. Some kinds of stress-induced impairments are even be reversible. In studies involving people between ages eighteen and fifty, our most generative years in terms of brain plasticity, Dr. Rajita Sinha, director of the Yale Stress Center, showed that intervention can turn the course on stress-induced cognitive impairment.

And in a study of medical students cramming long-term for an important licensing board exam, Conor Liston and his colleagues found that the students suffered from pronounced defi-

---

[34] Ibid.

[35] Center on the Developing Child at Harvard University: www.developingchild.harvard.edu.

[36] Ibid.

cits in the prefrontal cortex and scored poorly on a mental flexibility test. But just a month later, both the students' brain functioning and their performance had returned to normal.

As for the proposition of living a life of *no stress*, in another compelling experiment—this time involving female caregivers for husbands suffering from dementia—Dhabhar showed that moderate, transient stress was actually *healthier* than periods of low to no stress. What constitutes moderate, transient stress? How about exercise, which is widely seen as a stress reliever, but is in fact an acute stressor. This may seem like a contradiction, but consider how exercise may activate, in short spurts, the same biological response as running into a predator in the jungle. As such, the physical exertion of exercise represents a synergistic form of relief.[37]

A Road Map

The research and stories in the coming chapters paint a very different picture of stress—and living with stress—than the one that reverberates in the echo chamber of our culture. They help transform our narrative of stress from an all-encompassing punishment to skill building in the course of individual evolution and growth. The key to taking advantage of stress—to using stress as a road map to greater serenity, to more joy, passion and purpose, to better physical and psychological health—is to first begin understanding it across a spectrum that differentiates between constructive and destructive stress.

And the three most important markers on this map are your perceptions, your stories and your breaks, buffers and other protective factors.

---

[37] Sainani, "What, Me Worry?"

Observe and master your perceptions. "See yourself see." Your perception is the translator of your every moment. We must work hard to create a better framework for interpreting daily challenges. Stress and discomfort can serve as the doorway to life's greatest blessings. Shift your perception to interpret inevitable challenges in a way that serves you.

Tell the best stories. Your stories are collections of your perceptions and your perceptions, in turn, form your stories. It can be a virtuous—or vicious—cycle. Become conscious of detrimental cultural and personal narratives around stress and how they impact your mindset, language and actions. Embrace a narrative that casts stress as a pathway to adaptation and growth. Interpret (or reinterpret) challenging situations as motivators that lead the way to increased and enhanced performance, and as guides that open up new worlds and possibilities. Place a narrative around longer-term stress, rendering it tolerable and even important.

Commit to breaks, buffers and protective factors. Envision every day as a series of peaks and valleys. Vow to traverse both terrains in equal measure. Take concrete steps to incorporate breaks and buffers into your day in order to minimize and neutralize the adverse impact of chronic stressors. Limit the duration of stressful episodes by interspersing periods of acute stress with periods of low or no stress. Engage in creativity, passion, purpose and play. Laugh. Volunteer. Belong. Meditate. Read. Enjoy your loved ones. Spend your money in ways that will make you happier. Think. Learn. Ask why . . . a lot.

CHAPTER FIVE

A New Narrative

Live life as if everything is rigged in your favor.

—RUMI

The Athlete's Mindset

Some of the most compelling research and training to help prepare people to better handle stress involves athletes. Athletes can teach us a lot about using stress as a guide to thriving because for them, performance under high stress is a must, albeit for very different reasons. But the innovations being used to train athletes—including the beneficial narratives that propel them forward—could benefit the rest of us as well.

Michael Gervais is a Los Angeles–based high-performance psychologist. His job is to work with some of the world's top athletes, helping them to develop strategies not only to perform better, but to thrive under extreme pressure. At the core of Gervais's work is creating a new narrative of stress for the athletes he trains.

Gervais teaches his clients that there are two ways to view change: *eustress*,[38] change that you see as being positive, or *distress*, change that you view as negative. What's most important in any situation that causes anxiety is that the performer—the person going through the stress—can determine for him- or herself whether the change is in the eustress or distress category. When we perceive something as being eustressful, that stress helps us. Yet when we feel distressed, we need greater reserves of physical and emotional energy to regain balance.

Imagine you're a pro skier staring down a sixty-foot cliff, feeling the weight of the moment, the stakes of the outcome. One possible narrative for stress in that moment might be: "I shouldn't have stayed up late. I wish I had done more in the gym. These skis feel off." Gervais calls this a destructive dialogue. His training with athletes allows them to take a breath in that moment and to acknowledge the discomfort, but not to remain there. Gervais trains the athletes to feel the stress and then move through it to turn the energy, and the mental conversation into a position of strength—perhaps something like: "This discomfort is energizing. This is what I do. It's what I'm trained to do. I've done this my whole life. Let's go!" Gervais's mantra is that pain is both brilliant and necessary. This eventually becomes the mantra of the athletes he trains.

"Life is difficult," wrote M. Scott Peck in *The Road Less Traveled*. "This is a great truth, one of the greatest truths. It is a great truth because once we truly see this truth, we transcend it. Once we truly know that life is difficult—once we truly understand and accept it—then life is no longer difficult. Because once it is accepted, the fact that life is difficult no longer matters."

---

[38] Ironically, it was Hans Selye who coined the term "eustress" to indicate a positive response to a stressor.

One of our strongest motivators is to avoid pain and find a sense of comfort. And in seeking to avoid pain, we often find ourselves lost in a circuitous maze of more pain, more stress and more discomfort. We forget, perhaps, the sage words of Robert Frost that "the best way out is always through."[39] Or even the refrains from a beloved and enduring children's tale: "We can't go over it. We can't go under it. We've got to go through it!"[40]

What Gervais has found by working with some of the best and brightest athletes in the world is that they tend to do the exact opposite of avoiding. They don't seek to go under it or over it. They willingly move through situations that test their limits and extend their boundaries. Elite athletes make themselves uncomfortable and they stay in that space of discomfort as long as they can, in order to force a new adaptation of the way they respond. That's a very different way of looking at performing. It's also a very different way of looking at stress, anxiety and even suffering.

Gervais's training helps athletes create entirely new stories about stress, stories that recast stress as an amazing gift—one that sharpens our minds and heightens our focus.

"All stress means," he says, "is that we are engaging in change. Everyone wants to *grow*, but somehow no one wants to *change*. But you can't have one without the other."

This is an exciting proposition: a new way to tell our stories, to recast the very obstacles that seem to be in the way of our happiness as *the way* to happiness.

Is this sort of mindset a luxury afforded only to the elite? Hardly.

---

[39] Robert Frost, "A Servant to Servants."

[40] Michael Rosen, *We're Going on a Bear Hunt.*

Moving Toward a New Set of Rules

This book is not a guide to getting rid of stress, but a guide to getting *better and smarter* at stress, by understanding it, embracing it and using it. It challenges the prevailing idea that stress is an unrelenting plight. Toxic stress may well contribute to disease, both physical and mental, but the complete story of stress is far more nuanced and, in many ways, far more hopeful than the way most of us tend to see it now. We need to be able to put stress in its proper context.

A new narrative of stress must emerge: stress as a teacher, as a driver for growth, as a guide for how we should be living. The narrative reflects and synthesizes the mutually reinforcing works of both our master scientists and our spiritual masters. It represents a new way of thinking about stress, yet is also a timeless principle. It operates on dual planes of the practical and the ethereal. This new narrative is eminently practical as a way to confront the realities of the age in which we live. And yet it represents a shift in thinking about stress that is fundamental, seismic. It is sure to make many uncomfortable, and that discomfort is fine—important, even.

Stress can be our guide, if we let it. It can make us stronger, smarter and ultimately wiser and more balanced. It can push us to change and adapt. *How we think about stress is the key to unlocking its power.*

This abstract notion of becoming conscious of our stories and the subjectivity of our perceptions may sound like the stuff of philosophy or science fiction. But human perceptions and the ramifications of them are very real and potentially life changing. Consider the role perception plays in helping patients improve in all sorts of ailments, from pain and depression to Parkinson's disease, through the beneficial placebo effect. And consider also the lesser-known, opposite tendency, the nocebo effect. We must switch from the nocebo of stress to the placebo of stress, from a stress mindset to a growth mindset.

How might we harness the power of perception to live more conscious lives and, perhaps, to recast even the most dire situations in which we find ourselves?

How important are our stories? They are paramount. Because, in the end, what we are fighting for is also our imagination—the right to imagine lives and relationships and a world that is happier, less anxious, more harmonious and more just. We must fight for our stories, because a key tenet of freedom itself is indeed being able to imagine something better, more joyful and more fulfilling.[41]

The fundamental principle here is choice. It's not what happens to us, but how we choose to react that is important. Adversity may or may not be out of our control, but we do have control over our stories: what we tell ourselves and others about our circumstances, and how we choose to respond to them.

This is where we have complete control, a full range of potential actions to help us. We just need to focus on selecting the best responses for us. In order to do so, we need the proper tools: the right map, a well-calibrated compass and a well-functioning vessel.

And that is where our ten rules come in.

---

[41] Professor Ruha Benjamin, Princeton University.

PART TWO

STRESS AS A GUIDE

Your beliefs become your thoughts,
Your thoughts become your words,
Your words become your actions,
Your actions become your habits,
Your habits become your values,
Your values become your destiny.

—MAHATMA GANDHI

THE ROAD MAP

Constrain, adapt and advance, rendering stress tolerable and important.
- Shift perceptions to interpret inevitable challenges in a way that serves us better.
- Embrace a narrative that casts stress as a pathway to adaptation and growth.
- Commit to breaks, buffers, and protective practices that will minimize and neutralize the adverse impact of toxic stressors.

THE RULES	KEY TAKEAWAYS
I. YOUR WORLD	
BE RESILIENT	Cultivate optimism. Increase mental agility. Seek self-awareness. Self-regulate. Focus on strengths. Develop better connections. Encourage post-traumatic growth through storytelling. Engage in expressive writing to heal.
BELONG	Seek and engage in activities that encourage social bonding and companionship. Nurture a more expansive view of human relationships and groups. Work to constrain the meaning of negative experiences. Reframe narratives of exclusion and not belonging: "It's not just me. I'm not alone. Others feel this way too. This will pass."
BE CREATIVE	Nurture creativity. Become aware of the creativity bias. In stressful circumstances, attempt to approach problems in new and innovative ways. During times of greatest uncertainty and difficulty, embrace creativity to uncover new solutions. Use creativity to reframe your perception of events. Use techniques to help you become comfortable with uncertainty.
BE FREE	Remain open to the fact that stressful life circumstances can lead to change and that calamities can force us to "free" ourselves from rote, detrimental habits and expectations. Become more willing to "go down the rabbit hole." In times of great stress or difficulty, free yourself from preconceived notions and expectations to arrive at the best outcome and growth. Believe in your power. Walk the path to innovation and freedom.

II. YOUR MIND

BE HAPPY	Become conscious of how you define success.
	Choose intrinsic motivations over extrinsic ones.
	Become mindful of social, media and marketing messages.
	Redefine happiness as meaning and service.
BE GIVING	Spend money on others rather than on yourself.
	Underindulge rather than overindulge.
	Support people and charities.
	Create surprises.
	Buy experiences, not gifts.
	Buy time.
	Pay now, consume later.
BE KIND	Take responsibility for the energy you put into the world.
	Stand up or develop indifference.
	Reframe or change how you see things.
	Limit your exposure.
	Practice radical kindness.

III. YOUR BODY

BE HEALTHY	Heed the food-mood connection.
	Anticipate cravings.
	Work to create new reward pathways.
	Use habit to your advantage.
	Eat for optimal performance.
	Use healthy eating hacks.
BE UNCLUTTERED	Tackle one flat surface at a time.
	Find a place for everything, or purge.
	Become mindful of bringing in new things.
	Figure out your triggers.
	Get another perspective.
	Find your own balance.
	Begin practicing.

IV. WORLD, MIND AND BODY

BE PRESENT	The practice of mindfulness is an imperative for our ability to tackle a fast-moving new world.
	Use mindfulness to heal and transform the brain, and its ability to cope in stressful situations.
	Don't get caught up in definitions of meditation.
	Begin as simply as possible: with a one-moment meditation.

The New Rules

We are living in an era of great dissonance, of dramatic highs and lows, with lives that move at a pace and intensity impossible at any other time in history. These contradictions throw us off-kilter, out of harmony and balance. The problem, however, is not the havoc we might experience out in the world—life itself will always be a series of fluctuations: the good days, the bad days, the excruciating days—but *the way* we experience it. We cannot control what happens, but we can influence our stories, perceptions and physiology. This is the key to finding balance. It is the key to understanding and managing stress to your advantage.

The past several decades have seen an explosion of scientific research about stress and the fundamental building blocks of a meaningful and joyful life. In the coming chapters, we will explore ten principles that lie at the intersection of the science of stress and happiness, philosophy and spiritual writings.

These ten rules represent a carefully curated list from a diverse range of sources: many are traditional and others somewhat unusual. You will find that the bibliography skews in favor of big-picture articles and essays (rather than individual studies) by thoughtful writers—scientists and non-scientists—who do a great job of synthesizing a body of knowledge. A life spanning many continents, cultures and callings has taught me that the greatest lessons come from the most unlikely sources, and I have honored this principle in these pages. At the end of the book, you will find an appendix of selected sources with a list of books, essays, blogs, videos, audio and other resources. I invite you to continue the journey.

Our ten rules are divided into three categories: Your World, Your Mind and Your Body, each representing a crucial gateway to a life of balance and well-being. The final rule traverses all three. I debated (and flipped) the order of these categories for a long time before I settled on the current form, and here's why:

Your World: As we saw in Part One, so much of how we experience stress has to do with the way we perceive what happens to us and how we construct meaning from those experiences. The big picture of stress, therefore, is about the world we create for ourselves through the stories we tell. We can shift and optimize our perception of stress by changing how we see the world and how we relate to it.

Your Mind: A meaningful discussion of the downsides of stress requires that we examine our personal and cultural definitions of happiness and success. The way we think about these concepts and execute them in our lives can have a profound impact on our balance and well-being.

Your Body: It is said that the first home of a person's soul is the body and the second home, the house. We must focus on the ways of preparing our bodies and physical surroundings to optimally deal with stressors that come our way.

To extend the metaphor of our journey, these three sections will help us pull together our map of the world, calibrate our compass and prepare our vessel for adventure.

The lines between the three are not always clearly drawn, but these convenient if slightly artificial groupings will allow us to explore the concepts in a methodical fashion. And though our rules are laid out separately, they are mutually reinforcing and synergistic.

The strategies outlined in these rules will help us master stress in the everyday, but the benefit extends far beyond that. For some time now, a growing number of thought leaders from a variety of disciplines have been pointing to a seismic shift under way in our world. In *A Whole New Mind*, author Daniel Pink observes that we are entering a new age, "animated by a different form of thinking and a new approach to life." The convergence of the science of stress and happiness, philosophy and age-old spiritual wisdom validates this shift by showing us that a great deal of what we define as "stress" is due to growing pains, as we evolve beyond quickly deteriorating cultural and cognitive constructs that no longer work for us. The road map in this book, therefore, is instructive not just on how to interpret stress in the current moment but how to transition with mastery into this new world. This is how stress also becomes the road to serenity, to a life of purpose, empathy, creativity and bliss.

CHAPTER SIX

Your World

I knew that if I allowed fear to overtake me, my journey was doomed. Fear, to a great extent, is born of a story we tell ourselves, and so I chose to tell myself a different story from the one [we] are told. I decided I was safe. I was strong. I was brave. Nothing could vanquish me. Insisting on this story was a form of mind control, but for the most part, it worked. Every time I heard a sound of unknown origin or felt something horrible cohering in my imagination, I pushed it away. I simply did not let myself become afraid.

Fear begets fear.

Power begets power.

I willed myself to beget power.

And it wasn't long before I actually wasn't afraid. I was working too hard to be afraid.

—CHERYL STRAYED, *Wild*

Rule 1

Be Resilient

That which does not kill us makes us stronger.

—FRIEDRICH NIETZSCHE

I am fundamentally an optimist. Whether that comes from nature or nurture, I cannot say. Part of being optimistic is keeping one's head pointed toward the sun, one's feet moving forward. There were many dark moments when my faith in humanity was sorely tested, but I would not and could not give myself up to despair. That way lays defeat and death.

—NELSON MANDELA

Major Rhonda Cornum, pilot and flight surgeon with the 101st Airborne Division, arrived in Saudi Arabia in August 1990 at the height of Operation Desert Shield. Accompanied by her comrades, all of them in full military regalia, she stepped off the plane into what she thought was the hot jet blast. But she soon realized the blast of hot air was just the wind blowing. It was 130 degrees. "It was environmentally challenging," she would recall years later.

Six months after she arrived, a Black Hawk carrying Major Cornum and seven men on a search-and-rescue mission was shot down. As bullets flew, the soldiers on board followed protocol and jumped on Cornum, who was the flight surgeon. They were attempting to protect her, but since the bullets were coming from below, she was probably protecting *them*. Cornum was a pro. She knew all about helicopter crashes. And as their helicopter spun out of control, she was certain it would be an unsurvivable crash. The Apache pilot following the Black Hawk reported that the aircraft had exploded into a fireball upon impact. The crew was presumed lost.

When Cornum came to, she was staring at the wrong end of five AK47s. She and two others aboard the Black Hawk were severely injured, but they had survived. Cornum and Sergeant Troy Dunlap, another survivor, were placed on an Iraqi army truck to Basra. While bumping along a dark desert road in the back of the truck, an Iraqi soldier unzipped Cornum's flight suit and began sexually assaulting her. With a bullet in her back, two broken arms, a broken finger and a blown ligament in her knee, she was in no position to fight back.

Cornum was held prisoner for eight days and released a week after the war ended. When I spoke to her years later, she was matter-of-fact about the tragedy. "Look," she told me. "I wouldn't have chosen it. But since it did happen, I chose how I was going to respond to it." Cornum's words echoed those of Viktor Frankl's a half century earlier. Between stimulus and response, she found a space where her power, growth and freedom lay. She seized her power to choose her response. Cornum said she made an effort not to dwell on her disadvantage, but instead chose to turn it into an advantage. And through the years, she stayed true to that decision, including during her treatment for and recovery from breast cancer years later.

Rhonda Cornum is now a brigadier general, an MD and PhD whose slim exterior and casual bearing belies a steel strength bolstered by wisdom, character and grit. She is a remarkable woman to all who know her—one who embodies a certain scrappiness in the best sense of the word, a kind of blessed resilience.

I met General Cornum through Martin Seligman, a psychologist, educator and author who also happens to be known as the "father of positive psychology." Ironically, it was after decades of studying failure and helplessness that Dr. Seligman founded the field of positive psychology and devoted his career to learning more about positive emotions and character traits, including resilience and optimism, and the institutions that enable them.

Seligman observes that the human response to extreme stress and adversity is bell shaped. On one end of the spectrum are those with a bad, long-lasting reaction to a setback, and who will suffer from depression, anxiety and post-traumatic stress disorder, and be at higher risk for suicide. In the middle are the vast majority of people, who are mostly resilient. They may go through a very hard time for a short period, but within months they bounce back—by physical and psychological measures—to where they were before the crisis. On the other end are those who will suffer a major stress but who will emerge from the trauma much stronger. This is known as "post-traumatic growth." As a whole, human beings are more or less capable of coping with adversities. A subset of us, however, is gifted at it, and the interesting reasons why provide a brilliant framework for understanding and approaching stressful situations in a constructive way.[42]

---

[42] Martin Seligman, "Building Resilience," *Harvard Business Review*, April 2011.

The Curious Case of Post-traumatic Growth

Social scientist Emilia Lahti began studying sisu, a Finnish principle that dates back five centuries, after surviving an abusive relationship. It was in those crushing moments of adversity, when she felt she was being taxed beyond her mental and physical capacity, that Lahti began to contemplate how humans forge the strength necessary to overcome significant obstacles and stressors. The questions led her back to the culture in which she had grown up. Sisu is a source of pride for the Finns, but its meaning has been somewhat elusive. It stands for extraordinary determination and courage in the face of extreme adversity. It's the ability to endure significant stress, while taking action against seemingly impossible odds and transforming formidable obstacles into frontiers. This remarkable capacity makes an appearance again and again in a diverse range of cultures: The Jewish Wisdom Texts, for example, speak of *lechatchila ariber*, which encapsulates the same message.

It may not come as a surprise that Lahti began her study of sisu at the University of Pennsylvania, home to the Positive Psychology Center founded by Seligman and his colleagues. A number of gifted researchers have done seminal work in studying resilience and post-traumatic growth. Most anyone you stop on the street has heard about post-traumatic stress disorder, or PTSD. But mention post-traumatic *growth* and you are likely to be met with blank stares. Post-traumatic growth—the ability not only to bounce back from adversity but also to flourish—is an ever-present theme in our epic tales and spiritual traditions.

In the late 1960s Seligman and his colleagues discovered a phenomenon known as "learned helplessness," when they subjected animals to "mildly painful shocks" over which they had no control and could not escape. The animals eventually stopped trying to avoid the shocks. Later, even when there was an opportunity to escape, the animals behaved as if they were helpless and took no action to change their circumstances.[43]

Seligman would go on to show that humans experience learned helplessness in the same way as animals. But he observed something else that struck him as strange: Roughly one-third of the test subjects who experienced inescapable stimuli never became helpless. They continued trying to escape their plight. This piqued Seligman's interest. What was it that made them never give up?

Decades of research have shown that the most resilient among us—those who recover and go on to thrive following trauma—tend to be optimists. They see setbacks and bad events as *transient, temporary* and *changeable*. In humans, learned helplessness becomes a vicious loop of passivity and negative thought patterns, in which a person feels powerless to change a situation even when the situation is changeable. Optimists never really become helpless. And as a whole, optimists do much better reacting to trauma than pessimists, who are more likely to get stuck in learned helplessness.[44]

This gave Seligman clues as to how we might be able to immunize people against learned helplessness, against destructive thought patterns, and against giving up after failure: by teaching them resilience.

The Penn Resiliency Program, under the direction of psychologists Karen Reivich and Jane Gillham of the University of Penn-

---

[43] Seligman, "Building Resilience."

[44] Study by Martin Seligman and Steve Maier, quoted in Seligman, "Building Resilience."

sylvania, has since been replicated in diverse settings throughout the world.[45] The program had great success in reducing stress, anxiety and depression. Which is how Marty Seligman and Rhonda Cornum came to work together.

Master Resilience Training for Soldiers

Marty Seligman's path crossed General Cornum's when she began to look for ways to promote resilient thinking and prevent suicides in the military. For years Cornum had been advocating that the military improve soldiers' psychological fitness, instead of focusing on treatment after trauma had already occurred. After all, she reasoned, you don't teach people how to use their weapons after they're shot. She suspected from her experience that resilience could be learned. "You train and train and train until it's second nature. And then, when there's a crisis, you are prepared," she said.

The Penn Resiliency Program turned out to be a great fit, and so in 2009 Cornum undertook an important collaboration with Seligman and Reivich to establish resilience training for soldiers and their families. The resulting initiative, Comprehensive Soldier and Family Fitness, is a $145 million program that trains thousands of soldiers, family members and related civilians. One of the program's main components is designed to teach individuals how to embrace resilience in their own lives and then to pass on the knowledge to others.

Program co-director Karen Reivich told me that many people erroneously believe that if you are not born with the right genetic predisposition, resilience is out of reach. But research shows this to be false. Resilience is not just an advantage of a lucky few. It

---

[45] Penn Resiliency Program, www.ppc.sas.upenn.edu/prpsum.htm.

comprises a set of skills that, with effort, anyone can acquire. Specifically, it is made up of six basic building blocks: optimism, mental agility, self-awareness, self-regulation, character strengths and better connections.[46]

Reivich shared the six essential components of the Master Resilience Training. They are central to the perception and story-telling elements of constructive stress.

➤ **Cultivate optimism.** Optimism means believing that good things can happen and that you can effect positive change in your life and in the world. Pessimists underestimate how much control they have. They tend to focus their mental energy on things they can't do anything about. They also often hold the belief that optimists are either inauthentically exuberant or have their heads in the sand. In reality, though, most optimists can accurately assess what's going on; they just choose to place their attention on where they have control and on the positive aspects of situations.

Optimism takes effort. For many of us, says Reivich, it's easier to navigate toward and get consumed by the negative. But with some mindfulness, you can direct your attention toward the positive and what you can control. It is a habit that can be developed.

A simple way to help boost optimism is to pay closer attention to the good things, perhaps by keeping a gratitude journal. People who make a habit of gratitude sleep better, report greater life satisfaction, and have less depression and stress. In resilience training, Reivich and her team have people write down three good things that happen each day, then describe what they meant to them and how they might replicate the positive experiences the next day.

---

[46] Karen Reivich, *The Resilience Factor*, and Seligman, "Building Resilience."

➤ **Increase mental agility.** Mental agility is the ability to see situations fully, accurately and from multiple perspectives—an important skill to avoid that spiral of anxiety-inducing or negative thoughts when something goes wrong. These so-called thinking traps limit your flexibility by causing you to see only a small aspect of what's going on. Two of the more common thinking traps are the "me-me-me trap" (the tendency to always blame yourself) and the "them-them-them trap" (always blaming others). The key here is to identify which thinking trap you usually fall into and to develop your ability to see the other side. According to Reivich, once you become aware of the trap, you can hit the pause button and repeat a mantra to help you get a more accurate and flexible grasp of the situation. The catchphrase for the "me-me-me trap," for example, is "look outward."

➤ **Seek self-awareness.** Self-awareness helps you to understand your emotional habits so you can ask yourself, "How's that working for me?" Analyze your interpretation of adverse circumstances to figure out your internal dialogue under stress. One simple way to exercise self-awareness is to keep a journal of your thoughts during stressful periods. "When something triggers you—an activating event as little as not getting a parking spot or as big as losing a loved one—where does your mind go?" Reivich asks. "We teach people to look for patterns. Does your brain start sending out themes like 'loss,' 'danger' or 'trespass'? These patterns are like the glasses that color the way you see all events in your life—good and bad."

➤ **Self-regulate.** Self-regulation means learning how to respond to potential stressors in a calm, rational way. It's too easy to engage in unproductive thinking by assuming the worst. Reivich calls the phenomenon "making a Himalaya out of a mountain." It's something, but you make it bigger. The downward spiral of negative, catastrophic thinking makes you feel out of control. The problem then becomes a runaway train and creates huge anxiety. And that blocks purposeful action.

An exercise called "putting it in perspective" may help. First make three columns on a piece of paper. Record all the possible catastrophic results of a certain situation under the worst-case-scenario column. Next, write down the wildly unlikely best-case scenarios. And finally, list the most likely outcomes. This short exercise may help you assess the situation more accurately and dramatically shift your ability to tackle what's in front of you.

➤ **Focus on strengths.** Identify your top character strengths, whether it's your bravery, wisdom, sense of humor, or the ability to love and be loved. According to Reivich, people can usually tell you what their strengths are and who they are at their best. Those who stay resilient in the face of adversity use these strengths to overcome challenges. In doing so, they feel energized, motivated and true to themselves.[47]

➤ **Develop better connections.** One of the biggest myths about resilience is that it's a solitary sport. Resilience training provides tools for positive communication, with the key message that relying on others is necessary and is in no way a sign of weakness.

Most of us believe that the quality of our relationships is determined by the answer to the question "Will you be there for me when things go wrong?" But psychologist Shelly Gable's research shows that the real question is, "Will you be there for me when things go right?"

People typically respond in one of four ways to good news,

---

[47] You can take Penn's VIA Survey of Character Strengths (and a number of other related tests) by registering for free at www.authentichappiness.com.

and only one of those ways—active and constructive responding—strengthens our relationships: First we have the conversation killer—"That's great!" as you're texting or on the computer. Then there's the conversation hijacker—"That reminds me of my good news!" And the joy thief—"But what about . . . ?" with a list of the downsides.

Finally we have the joy multiplier, who asks questions, offers praise, favors the positive experience, and is authentically interested in the details. The beauty is that multiplying joy is not hard to do. It just requires intention and attention.

Also key to developing better connections: effective praise. Research by Stanford psychologist Carol Dweck underscores the value of specific, authentic praise, as compared to generalities. Reivich and her colleagues also teach assertive communication, and how the language, voice tone, body language and pace of assertive communication vary from their far less constructive passive and aggressive counterparts.[48]

Ultimately, none of the resilience skills Reivich and her colleagues teach are difficult. They're basic tried-and-true principles echoed through much of our culture. What they do require is mindfulness—and practice.

Resilience Through Storytelling

In a way, extreme stress is self-fulfilling. The key is to switch the focus of both our perceptions and stories to post-traumatic growth. Some people naturally switch the focus of the narrative. Others can engage in a narrative storytelling model developed by Dr. James Pennebaker.

---

[48] Seligman, "Building Resilience."

The idea of a fundamental human need for self-expression is reflected in Dr. Pennebaker's two decades of research. Pennebaker, professor of psychology at the University of Texas at Austin, is a pioneer in the study of using expressive writing as a route to healing. Early in his career he stumbled across a correlation between people who had had traumatic experiences and increased health problems. He became fascinated by the damaging nature of secrets.

Pennebaker says that major stressors in life influence physical health and may lead to potentially devastating biological changes, including elevations in cortisol, immune disruption, cardiovascular changes and a cascade of neurotransmitter changes. Secrets only turn up the pressure that much more.[49]

Pennebaker wondered early on what would happen if he brought people into the lab and asked them to reveal the traumas they had kept secret. In his first study, published in 1986, he randomly assigned subjects to write either about major upheavals or about superficial topics. In the six months that followed, those who had written about trauma visited doctors at much lower rates than those who had written about random topics. In another study in the 1990s on people with AIDS, those who wrote about their diagnosis and how it had affected their lives experienced a beneficial increase in white blood cell counts and a drop in their viral loads. Study after study bore out Pennebaker's thesis that putting negative experiences into words has positive physical and psychological effects.

In time he began to see nuances in the way writing helps us heal. People who were able to make a positive slant in their writing—by using words like "love," "care," "happy" and "joy"—

---

[49] See James W. Pennebaker and Cindy K. Chung, "Expressive Writing: Connections to Physical and Mental Health."

appeared to benefit more than others. "Even if the person was saying, 'No one cares about me' or 'I don't love anyone,' that still meant they're thinking about a dimension of happiness. It's better to say you're not happy than to say you're sad," says Pennebaker.

Another important factor was an element of self-reflection in the writing, often manifested through the use of causal words like "because," "cause," "effect," "reason," "rationale" or any other word that suggested the writer was trying to make sense of what happened. "If you're telling the same story over and over again, you won't benefit and your friends will go crazy," notes Pennebaker. "It's putting things together, the cause and effect, the self-reflection that makes a difference."

The ability to shift perspective is also key. Standing back and seeing trauma from different points of view—your own and through the eyes of others—is a marker of a better psychological state.

Feel Guilt, Not Shame

Research by George Mason University psychology professor June Tangney introduces an important nuance to the way we tell our stories by demonstrating the difference between guilt and shame, and their impact on resilience. Tangney studies "self-conscious emotions," a group to which guilt and shame belong, alongside pride and embarrassment. Self-conscious emotions require recognizing the self as separate from others, and reflecting upon this individual self in reference to some internal or societal standards.

According to Tangney, though most people tend to use guilt and shame interchangeably, they are quite different. These emotions give rise to dramatically different feelings, motivations and behaviors. When people feel guilty, they feel bad about a specific behavior. When they feel shame, however, they are usually feeling bad about themselves, believing not just that they've done wrong, but that they are a bad person. There is a sense of shrinking, a sense of being worthless and/or powerless. Not only do shamed people feel exposed; they are acutely tuned in to the fact that other people may be judging them. As such, they are more inclined to deny or attempt to hide and escape the situation.

Guilt, though also an unpleasant emotion, is nowhere near as overwhelming as shame. Tangney's research shows that while guilt-ridden people often feel tension, remorse and regret, they are far more focused on confessing, apologizing and reparation. Shamed people feel bad about themselves, she says, but guilty people are more likely to be thinking about their effect on others.

Studies show that people who are prone to guilt are more forgiving. They handle anger more constructively, experience more empathy and have a greater ability to see others' perspectives. Those prone to shame, on the other hand, are more likely to hold grudges and are less likely to forgive when they feel wronged. Shame is also associated with feelings of anger and aggression and the tendency to blame others.

Guilt can be a good thing, a highly beneficial and adaptive emotion, observes Tangney. Shame, however, is too personal. In other words, there are good ways and bad ways to feel bad.

How do you switch from a destructive narrative of shame to the far more constructive guilt narrative? Begin by learning to differentiate between the two. Tangney says that understanding the difference between shame and guilt, so you can recognize when you are feeling shame, can make a big difference.

A Better Narrative

During a routine physical exam in the early 1990s, Chris Klug found out that his blood tests showed abnormal liver functioning. He wasn't sure at the time what "abnormal" meant—whether it was good or bad. He did know, however, that his doctor wanted to get to the bottom of why his blood work was off. He was in his early twenties and, he thought, in perfect health. Klug was a professional athlete with a high-profile snowboarding career. But that initial diagnosis began a year and a half of being poked and prodded through a battery of tests.

It turned out to be a disease called primary sclerosing cholangitis, or PSC, an autoimmune disease that was destroying the bile ducts of his liver. He was told he would one day require a liver transplant.

The diagnosis did not compute. It struck Klug as surreal. He felt like a million bucks. As a world-class athlete, he was outdoors every day preparing for the upcoming Olympics, and yet now he was on a transplant waiting list. Being asymptomatic, he thought the doctors were nuts. Later he would realize that they had saved his life.

In 1998, Klug competed in the Olympics with his own liver. He placed sixth. By the spring of 2000, his health had begun to deteriorate and he was soon at death's door. He was upgraded to critical as he got sicker. He wondered if he would ever get the transplant call or if he would die waiting.

Those were dark days and nights, he remembers. He was humbled, but never hopeless.

On July 28, 2000, Chris Klug got the call: There was a liver available for him.

He remembers waking up in the hospital after the operation and thinking: *This is how it's supposed to feel!* "I knew right then that I was going to make it back," he says. "It was like a new engine was dropped in me—as if a light went on in me."

Four days after his operation, he was out of the hospital. Seven days later, he was riding a bicycle. Eighteen months later, he competed in the 2002 Olympic Games in Salt Lake City and brought home the bronze medal for the United States. Chris Klug became the first person to win an Olympic medal after surviving a liver transplant.

He credits his support network of family and friends for getting him through his illness and recovery. But there was something else too: "I refused to quit. I refused to give up. That was not a story I was willing to entertain." He asked himself: "Will I let this experience cause me to live a compromised lifestyle?" The answer, he decided, was no.

"I am an eternal optimist," he says. "My attitude was, I'm going to train for this transplant with everything in my power, both mentally and physically, to have a successful outcome. I was going to get back [in shape] and I didn't settle for anything else."

As terrifying as the ordeal was, Klug says the experience was the most positive in his life—it shaped him into who he is and made him realize what was important: his family, his friends and his faith. In 2004, Klug established a foundation dedicated to raising awareness about the importance of organ and tissue donation. He sees his ordeal as a lesson in how fragile life is and how to make the most of every twist and turn.

Practice

- **Write about your challenges.**
  Nancy Morgan, director of the Writing & Health Initiative at
  Georgetown Lombardi Cancer Center, provides the following
  guidelines for expressive writing.

  - Find a quiet moment and write about your thoughts and feel-
    ings continuously for at least twenty minutes. Don't be con-
    cerned about spelling or grammatical errors.

  - Describe how you feel about any stressful circumstances.

  - Write only for yourself.

  - Also write about something that makes you feel good, even if it's
    unrelated to your crisis: a memorable summer, perhaps, or a turn-
    ing point in your life, or a mentor who helped you out.

  - Trust that once you begin, your feelings most in need of release
    will find their way to the paper. Your writing may be a few sen-
    tences, or it may go on as long as you need it to. Deal only with
    what you can handle.

  - Later in the day, reflect on your writing experience. How did
    the writing make you feel?

- **Recognize and transform your stories and perceptions.**
  In her book, *Metaphor-phosis: Transform Your Stories from Pain to
  Power,* acupuncturist, herbalist, and author Lesley Tierra recommends
  writing to uncover the core beliefs, patterns and important story lines in
  our lives. Tierra observes that positive thinking and affirmations can
  help us transform our lives, "but because stories are dominated by
  subconscious patterns and beliefs, they ultimately control your life

regardless." The purpose of the following exercises is to shed light on these patterns, beliefs and stories, and to examine whether they serve us.

○ Write down the most important positive and negative beliefs you hold about yourself. Some examples may be: "I am all alone." "Everyone loves me." "I am the smartest person in the room" or "I'm bad at relationships" or "I never have enough money." Keep writing until you have run out of things you believe about yourself. Don't share this list with anyone. It is for you only, so that you may begin to observe and recognize some of the story lines that influence your everyday perceptions. Eventually, writes Tierra, "you'll come to see and understand that everything you say and do is a story, and that everything you hear and see is a story too."

○ Draw a timeline on a large sheet of paper. Mark it at the far left with your birth year and at the far right with the current year. Try to recall and mark on the timeline the most important events in your life, both the best and the worst, both high points and low points, from the most inconsequential to gravest, so long as the event is significant to you. After you finish, make a note of the patterns and story lines in your life. Tierra observes that "[i]f you are hooked by a story or pattern, you will react from the belief you hold. This is what you can adjust. You can discharge the energy from the pattern, release the story's hook, and choose to respond in another way."

○ Observe the way you interact with others. What do you think about and feel over and over when dealing with others? Tierra suggest making a list of the triggers, reactions and emotions that recur in your interactions. There is nothing inherently wrong with the stories we tell ourselves. It is crucial, however, to determine whether you are "bound, limited, hooked, or held back" by your stories or whether they serve you to "live your highest potential and greatest dreams." The very first step is self-awareness.

Rule 2
Belong

It was 2012, just a few days before graduation, and Yale senior Marina Keegan was contemplating her future.

"We don't have a word for the opposite of loneliness," she mused in an essay that was to be published in the Yale daily newspaper, "but if we did, I could say that's what I want in life. . . . It's not quite love and it's not quite community; it's just this feeling that there are people, an abundance of people, who are in this together."

Her yearning for the opposite of loneliness was simple enough. Her meditation on community spread quickly through social media, striking a chord among people around the world. It did so for two reasons:

The first was a visceral recognition of the truth she spoke about our human need to belong.

And the second was a profound sadness. By the time most people read her longing words on the "opposite of loneliness," Marina had died in a tragic car accident.

The impact of young Marina Keegan's death was a kind of collective awakening. Some even paused long enough from their busy lives to contemplate the question she had asked in the first place: What exactly is the opposite of loneliness?

All for One and One for All

It begins with belonging.

Belonging is not just a piece of the larger puzzle of what modern-day stress can teach us about how to live. It's far more important than that. One of the most robust protective factors for those experiencing toxic stress is community and a sense of social belonging.

We humans have an urgent need to belong: to one another, to our friends and families, to our culture and country, to our world.

Belonging can act as a key psychological lever with broad consequences. Our interests, motivation, health and happiness—our ability to live a joyful and meaningful life—are inextricably tied to the sense that we belong to a greater community.

The dark flipside of belonging—loneliness and isolation—turns out to be one of our most pernicious stressors that can wreak havoc on our bodies and minds, and lives.

Loneliness is painful. That it's also a risk factor for serious health problems on par with smoking cigarettes and worse than even obesity or leading a sedentry life sometimes may come as a shock. If you were to conduct an impromptu poll of risky behaviors, you might expect a list of the obvious ones, like smoking, eating junk food, inactivity or even depression. But loneliness?

And yet loneliness lords over the others exactly because it is so vital to our sense of happiness and well-being, for these in turn affect almost every aspect of our physical health, and how we deal with stress.

University of Chicago social psychologist John Cacioppo has pioneered much of our understanding about the harmful effects of loneliness. Cacioppo's research suggests that it's our subjective experience of loneliness—our perception—that's damaging and not our actual social contacts and support.

Loneliness is sometimes confused with social isolation. Though there is some overlap, the two are distinct. Social support is both the perception and act of being cared for. It can be measured through a number of characteristics, such as marital status, social network or participation in community activities like church.

But different people have different tendencies. Have you ever heard someone say, "I was standing in a crowded room, yet I was all alone?" Loneliness is the sense that you are no longer connecting with people. It's the quality and not the quantity that matters. Some of us are more introverted than others, content with just a close friend or two and preferring to have more alone time. Others are more extroverted and truly suffer without the companionship and support of scores of friends.

In his book, *Loneliness: Human Nature and the Need for Social Connection*, Cacioppo writes about the "genetic thermostat" for loneliness, calibrated differently for different people. Loneliness thus becomes "the gap between a person's *desired* and *actual* social relationships." Once again, your perception becomes key to the equation, since what is welcome solitude for one person may be devastating loneliness for another.[50]

So What's the Damage?

The damage of loneliness is broad and far-reaching, impacting both physical and mental health. In a general sense, feeling isolated dramatically elevates stress levels.

---

[50] John Cacioppo, *Loneliness: Human Nature and the Need for Social Connection*; Judith Shulevitz, "The Lethality of Loneliness," *New Republic*, May 13, 2013; Ray Hainer, "Loneliness Hurts the Heart," CNN Health, August 10, 2009.

Rejection—or even just the fear of rejection—is also profoundly damaging. Even a single instance of exclusion can undermine a person's sense of well-being, as well as cognitive factors such as IQ test performance, brain function, memory and learning, and self-control.

Studies show that if you feel a sense of social belonging related to a task, you will be motivated to continue working on it. You will persist even on the most challenging of tasks because you have the sense of a collective goal. The reverse is also true: If you don't feel like you belong, you are both less motivated and less likely to hang in there in the face of obstacles.

In social contexts like work or school, a sense of not belonging can be downright debilitating. Workplace and productivity expert and author Judith Glaser writes that feeling left out causes the person who has been excluded to become less productive, innovative and collaborative. "They feel threatened. Cortisol flows in. Their executive centers shut down. Behavior shifts from trust to distrust. And the effect can last for hours." Rejection alters the sufferer's perception so that she reveals less, expects more, assumes the worst and interprets context through fear and paranoia.[51]

Heartbreak, Literally

What country songs have been warning about all these years is true: Loneliness can break your heart in a very real sense. In recent years researchers have begun to pinpoint the biological effects of loneliness. Research by Cacioppo shows that chronic

---

[51] Judith E. Glaser, "Preventing Rejection at Work," *Harvard Business Review*, April 24, 2013.

solitude unleashes unhealthy changes in sufferer's cardiovascular, immune and nervous systems. The socially isolated have shorter life spans and a higher risk for a host of issues, from depression to infections, but in older adults, loneliness is also an unfortunate predictor for mortality.

While it may be surprising that the stress of loneliness appears to have such a distinct impact on the heart, researchers have in fact unraveled the distinct ways that different stressors cause stress to manifest. In one particularly sobering study, researchers questioned almost thirteen hundred patients preparing to undergo coronary artery bypass surgery about their health. Patients' ratings of one statement—"I feel lonely"—predicted dramatically higher mortality, both in the short and long term.[52]

The Belonging Intervention

In 2011 social psychologist Gregory Walton made waves by accomplishing what was acknowledged to be a remarkable feat: By putting a group of college freshmen through a simple one-hour exercise, he managed to cut in half the notorious academic achievement gap between the white and minority students participating in his study.

Cutting the academic achievement gap is a big deal. It is a stubbornly persistent educational disparity between the performance of white students and their minority counterparts, and it has dogged education activists for decades now. The achievement gap is not a function of just socioeconomics—children from af-

---

[52] John Cacioppo, *Loneliness: Human Nature and the Need for Social Connection.* See also Hainer, "Loneliness Hurts the Heart."

fluent families of color are as besieged by it as children from poorer families.

Professor Walton and his colleagues enlisted a group of university freshmen, roughly half of them African-American and the other half white. The students were told they would be serving as experts to help others who were going through a difficult time. Walton called his study "the belonging intervention."

"You will be helping a group of students who are lonely," the study participants were told. "They don't feel like they belong here."

The freshman students participating in the study read through a report that included statistics, quotations and stories from upperclassmen about their experiences in freshman year. The report revealed that most of the seniors had also struggled when they had first arrived at school, but eventually got through it.

The report emphasized that concerns about belonging were common, temporary, and due to "the challenging nature of college transition." Feeling lonely, as if you did not belong, was the same for everyone during that difficult first year, regardless of gender or ethnicity. For example, one of the quotes included in the report noted: "Freshman year, even though I met large numbers of people, I didn't have a small group of close friends . . . I was pretty homesick and I had to remind myself that making close friends takes time. Since then . . . I have met people, some of whom are now just as close as my friends in high school were."

The participants, who believed they were writing for the next generation of incoming freshmen—an audience many of them related to and cared about—began to engage with the material and use it to reflect on their own experiences, including how they had conquered the challenge of feeling left out.

In fact, the report the students used to write the essay was pure fiction. It had been crafted by Professor Walton and his colleagues. There were no lonely upperclassmen (at least, none that the researchers had interviewed). The researchers also had no plans to distribute the essays or videotaped interviews to any incoming freshmen. The study subjects, of course, had no idea about any of this. In parallel to these students was a control group who completed a similar task on the physical environment of the college.

The researchers then followed the students from the second semester of college until graduation.

For the white students, the study had little to no effect. But for the black participants, the academic outcomes were remarkable. The intervention, delivered in the first year of college, changed the trajectory of minority students' achievement, as they steadily improved their grades all the way through senior year. Over the next several years, they had higher grade point averages relative to multiple control groups. In the end, the minority achievement gap overall was reduced by a dramatic 50 percent. The belonging intervention tripled the percentage of African-American students who graduated in the top 25 percent of their class.

This was news enough on its own. But Walton's study also revealed something else entirely. The study's success was not just limited to a difference in academics and GPA. The intervention had also impacted the participants' stress levels. The African-American students in the study reported feeling more resilient in the face of daily stressors. Up to three years later, the black students who had gone through the belonging intervention continued to flourish. They reported themselves as being happier and healthier. What's more, those in the intervention group reported visiting the doctor 50 percent less than their control counterparts.

A one-hour-long belonging exercise in the first year of college had paid off handsomely *four years later.*

Professor Walton's research speaks volumes about the power

of the perception of belonging. The researchers observed that the intervention had helped downgrade uncontrollable stress by allowing the students to shift their perception and put a narrative around traumatic experiences. Key to the study's successful outcome had been a change in how the participants looked at their social situation. That is, the intervention had reduced the degree to which students correlated bad days with not belonging, by providing them with a nonthreatening framework for interpreting daily challenges.

"They had learned to place those experiences in a box," Walton told me, "with a beginning, a middle and an end. As a consequence, the meaning of the negative experience was constrained, and people understood that when bad things happened, it wasn't just them, they were not alone and that it was something that would pass."

Walton has gone on to replicate the belonging intervention in a number of different contexts, with preschoolers and middle schoolers, as well as with women in predominantly male disciplines. In scenario after scenario, the belonging intervention has had the same effect. His experiments serve as a powerful demonstration of the importance of community, and that if you can find ways to increase your sense of belonging, it impacts your well-being in profound and far-reaching ways.

Mere Belonging

Professor Walton's experiments show that the short answer to achieving "the opposite of loneliness" is *belonging*.

The short answer, yes, but by no means the easy answer. Human beings, desperate to be included, have also demonstrated an almost pathological knack for excluding others. The pathology of exclusion underpins some of our greatest social diseases: racism, homophobia and gender discrimination, to name just a few. Some scholars argue that the most divisive of our society's current controversies, particularly immigration and political empowerment, are best understood as questions over the politics of *belonging* in the United States and how the shifting dynamics of identity, race and ethnicity come into play. Entire wars are being fought over who belongs—and who doesn't.

This raises an important question: How profound does the sense of belonging have to be to reap its benefits?

The messages that Professor Walton's belonging intervention conveyed were not exceptional. Nor were they particularly complicated. "You are not alone," they said. "You belong. It gets better."

Perhaps the most important insight about belonging is that although we often think of group membership as a deep or longstanding connection, it doesn't *need* to be either. In a different series of experiments involving children, Walton and his colleagues showed that even a minimal social link to another person or group can still exert a powerful influence.

Walton's findings highlight how important group identity can be to both motivation and learning. They also confirm that people can develop socially shared motivations, and that "a mere sense of social connectedness" keeps us motivated to keep working on challenging tasks even in the absence of others.

Perhaps most curious about the study was this: The groups that had kept the study participants motivated and on task did not even exist! They had been made up! Again, what mattered was *perception*.[53]

---

[53] Annie Murphy Paul, "A Group Doesn't Even Have to Exist to Affect Our Behavior," Brilliant Blog, April 25, 2013, http://anniemurphypaul.com/2013/04/a-group-doesnt-even-have-to-exist-to-affect-our-behavior/#.

Mindfulness and Meditation

In a hyperconnected world, we may be tempted to cast a hopeful eye toward technology, and social networks in particular, as a potential savior from isolation. While many researchers have tried to use social networks to reduce loneliness in at-risk populations like older adults, the research is spotty—sometimes these approaches work, but often they don't. Study after study shows that social networks simply do not provide the health benefits of direct contact with other people.

A somewhat paradoxical way to counteract the stress of isolation is by altering our inner mental spaces, particularly through meditation. By doing so, we can cultivate a deliberate internal shift that changes our perception of the outer social environment.

Research conducted by Carnegie Mellon psychology professor David Creswell sheds light on how inner shifts can help counteract loneliness, by extending the known benefits of mindfulness-based meditation into previously uncharted territories: helping to reduce loneliness and the risk of disease in older adults.

Professor Creswell and his colleagues enlisted healthy older adults between the ages of fifty-five and eighty-five, and asked them to complete a questionnaire assessing their loneliness. The study participants were assigned randomly to one of two groups. The first group took part in an eight-week mindfulness-based stress reduction program that included two-hour skills training sessions each week, daily thirty-minute meditation exercises at home and a daylong retreat. The control group received no treatment.

Participating in the meditation program reduced the older adults' perceptions of loneliness compared with those of the control group, who experienced small increases in loneliness. Prior randomized controlled trials had found that the perception of loneliness was unaltered after the administration of social support and skills training. The researchers were thus able to attribute the results to the meditation practice, rather than to the fellowship afforded by being part of a research group or to other factors. In addition, other trials have shown that even when meditation is taught on a one-on-one basis, participants experience reductions in stress symptoms and improvements in physical health markers.

The scientists also made a second compelling discovery. Not only did the mindfulness-based stress reduction program decrease the participants' sense of loneliness, it significantly reduced proinflammatory gene expression and the amount of C-reactive protein (CRP) in their blood—both markers for chronic inflammation.

"It is amazing," Professor Creswell told me. "For the first time, we are seeing that a behavioral practice—paying attention to your experience from moment to moment—has the power to change the gene expression in your immune cells." He hypothesized that meditation helps people to not get caught up in the spiral of distress by simply providing a break in the day in which to disconnect from harmful thought patterns.

Mystical and contemplative traditions offer an alternate hypothesis for the same effect—that meditating can reconnect us with our universal oneness.

Neuroscientist Jill Bolte Taylor had the unique opportunity to experience the deterioration of her brain after a stroke in 1996. In a riveting TED talk and subsequent bestseller, she described how the left side of her brain shut down over the course of four hours, taking with it functions such as ego, analysis, judgment and context. As she became "disconnected" from her body, the brain chatter died down and she experienced a sense of peacefulness. With the muting of the left brain, she also shed the stresses of her life—her job, her schizophrenic brother and, as she put it, thirty-seven years of emotional baggage. She recalled it as a state of nirvana.[54]

Her description of the experience is especially compelling in the context of belonging. Taylor described her perception of her own physical boundary as no longer being limited to where her skin met air. "My entire self-concept shifted as I no longer perceived myself as a single, a solid, an entity with boundaries that separated me from the entities around me," she observed. "I now blended with the space and flow around me."

This description of the state of "oneness" is echoed throughout many of the world's religious and mystical writings. "All differences in this world are of degree and not of kind, because oneness is the secret of everything," wrote Hindu monk Swami Vivekananda.

Jill Bolte Taylor reached her nirvana through adversity. However, her description of the state of oneness is not far off from what others have achieved through mindfulness and spiritual discipline. The state of euphoria she describes parallels accounts in Christian, Buddhist, Kabbalistic and other mystical traditions of the state of oneness achieved through prayer and contemplation, mindfulness and meditation.

The poet and mystic Khalil Gibran wrote:

> You are my brother, and both of us are sons of a
> single, universal, and sacred spirit.
> You are my likeness, for we are prisoners of the same
> body, fashioned from the same clay.

---

[54] Leslie Kaufman, "A Superhighway to Bliss," *The New York Times*, May 25, 2008.

> You are my companion on the byways of life, my
>   helper in perceiving the essence of reality
>   concealed behind the mists.
> You are a human being and I have loved you, my
>   brother.

A Culture of Inclusion

Extrovert or introvert, we all thrive when connected and decline in the face of loneliness and isolation. Recognizing destructive patterns of rejection can help, both to provide perspective and to break such patterns where we can. So, too, can creating an awareness of our fundamental oneness and shared identity—our belonging, first and foremost, to one race of humanity.

The answer here lies not in denying our individuality, but in also nurturing a culture of kindness and inclusion. The shift toward inclusion begins with each of us every day. It begins with empathy, candor and caring, and breeds a virtuous cycle of trust, of belonging, of better health and happiness.

Dr. Taylor describes nurturing a culture of inclusion as a question of choice. Science has shown that our right brain is set up to focus on our similarities, the present moment and the bigger picture of how we are all connected. Our left brain, on the other hand, thinks linearly, creates and understands language, judges what is right and wrong, and is a "master of details, details and more details about those details."

The two sides of our brain work in harmony to provide both the emotional drive and the actionable steps to create positive change.

Do we have the power to choose being kind and inclusive over being judgmental and exclusive?

"Of course we do," writes Dr. Taylor, "and the better we understand the choices we have been making, either consciously or unconsciously, the more say we will have in the world we create." She points out: "Neurocircuitry may be neurocircuitry, but we don't have to run on automatic."[55]

So many of us operate from biased information. We have our own experiences and can see others only from the outside. And though we share many of the same difficulties, few reveal them outwardly.

When you feel isolated and depressed, you may wish to recall some powerful truths about being human:

It's not just you.

We are all struggling in one way or another.

You should not judge your insides by other people's outsides.

"It's not quite love," wrote young Marina Keegan, "and it's not quite community; it's just this feeling that there are people, an abundance of people, who are in this together."

Unity. In infinite diversity. With a separation that is only imagined.

And so we are.

Practice

- **Connect now.**
  To remedy your sense of isolation, try activities like volunteering, joining social and community groups, pet therapy and traditional counseling.

---

[55] Jill Bolte Taylor, "Does Our Planet Need a Stroke of Insight?" Huffington Post, January 3, 2013.

- **Try mindfulness.**

  Meditation and nostalgia have also been shown to help counteract loneliness and social isolation by shifting perceptions and helping to alter our mental inner spaces.

- **Think unity.**

  In the long term, nurturing a culture of inclusion can lead to a virtuous cycle of trust, belonging, better health and happiness.

Rule 3

Be Creative

Our goal should be to live life in radical amazement . . . Get up in the morning and look at the world in a way that takes nothing for granted. Everything is phenomenal. To be spiritual is to be amazed.

—RABBI ABRAHAM JOSHUA HESCHEL

There are lots of people who think Chicago's South Side is its toughest neighborhood, but Fernando Pullum maintains that it's the West Side that holds that distinction. Pullum grew up across the street from the Henry Horner projects. "Every two blocks there was a gang," he remembers. "And when school was dismissed, we all had to run home."

He was raised, off and on, by his great-grandmother because his parents were both drug addicts. His mother was a prostitute who sometimes worked across the street from his junior high. She was in and out of jail.

People express disbelief when he tells them that when he was a toddler his mother would hand him a list of things she needed from the store across the alley and tell him to go buy them on credit. "I was a baby, parenting my mother," he says. When he was four years old, the drug use got really bad. His mother, practically a child herself, began leaving his younger sister with him. So he started taking care of her as well. Sometimes, when his mother was in jail, he begged for food.

What Pullum remembers most about growing up is stress. All the time, deep and broad, so thick he couldn't see his way through. He fought every day—every single day, he says. His scarred and broken body now pays testament to those hard times: bones in his hand, healed and rehealed three times. Scars here and there. Knots on the back of his head.

He remembers the first defining moment when the light entered through the cracks of his fractured life: a scene in his grandmother's living room with a handful of relatives, all messing around on an old bugle that no one could manage to make a sound on. He picked it up and blew. It made a horrible sound, but it was a sound nonetheless and so unexpected that everyone broke into applause. That moment when everyone cheered was the first time he saw the light, but at least now he knew what it looked like and how it felt. So he started looking out for it.

There were many times of quiet despair, like when the relatives would openly say that he was going to grow up and spend his life in prison. Or the time his mother did not stand up to protect him from her pimp. "He was dangerous," Pullum says quietly. "He almost killed my mother."

During those times, he remembered the sound that the horn had made. He remembered the applause. He imagined what a different life might look like.

When he was in sixth grade, Pullum was in class when the school's band director walked into the room and said he needed a baritone player in the band. No one raised their hand. Except Pullum, who would have jumped at the chance to play anything. The band director kept overlooking him, on purpose, hoping someone else would volunteer. But Pullum kept jumping up and down, begging. The band director relented.

That instrument was so big, Pullum could barely carry it across the street, especially in the harsh Chicago winters when there was so much snow. He didn't care. Eventually the band director felt so sorry for Pullum, he switched him to a trumpet. That was when Pullum's world cracked wide open. He stayed after school every day and played and played and played as if his life depended upon it. And it did. When he played, Pullum disappeared from this world and appeared in another.

"You pick up your horn," he says, "and your color and your age and how much money you have and every bit of misery you have to live through—it all disappears. You enter a world that is an equal playing field for everyone. It is the only thing you can be judged by. When I was playing, I wasn't a poor black kid with drug-addicted parents. I was a musician. Transported."

That boy who was supposed to have been destined for prison found an entryway into this other realm, and even as he walked through it, horn in hand, he promised himself that he would come back for others like him. He graduated high school and went to Chicago State University as a commuter. He played music at night and went to school during the day. At the urging of the school's band leader, Pullum eventually transferred to the University of Michigan, where he was an honors student. When he graduated, the Michigan band director reminded Pullum to keep the door open for others.

In the decades that followed, Fernando Pullum played with Ella Fitzgerald, Stevie Wonder, Etta James, Jackson Browne, Alicia Keys and many others. He traveled the world. He met Prince Charles and President Ford, and many other dignitaries. Through it all, he taught music—in public schools, in community centers, on the streets, wherever he could. For some of those children, Pullum was that very first glimpse into what a different life might look like. And in 2011 he founded the Fernando Pullum Community Arts Center, in a Los Angeles neighborhood that reminded him very much of where he grew up.

•   •   •

Creativity is the cornerstone of our ability to respond effectively to our biggest stressors. It matters to our emotional well-being as we find our way in an uncertain, rapidly shifting world. Imagination helps us to remain resilient during difficult and stressful times since creative people tend to be more tolerant of ambiguity and better able to come back from defeat. Here, once again, we see the critical importance of storytelling to constructive stress. But we also encounter a key element of destructive stress: fear—specifically, the fear of uncertainty.

With the challenges we are facing both individually and collectively, we need to rethink and expand our conception of creativity. It is absolutely not a luxury and at no time in history has that been truer than now. Consciously or unconsciously, many of us place imagination and creativity within the tight boundaries of traditionally artistic endeavors—in itself something of a creative failure. David Kelley, founder of the design firm IDEO[56] and recognized as one of America's leading design innovators, told me once: "Creativity is not just about painting or drawing or art. It is about problem solving. It's the flexibility of your mind, the ability to see things that no one can see and envision something entirely different. We are creating the future, bringing about change. And there is something incredibly empowering about that."

---

[56] IDEO has been pivotal to the creative disruption of a slew of products, services, spaces and systems including, famously, Apple's first mouse.

MAKE magazine founding editor Dale Dougherty, honored by the White House as a Champion of Change, observed: "Our future security lies in knowing what we are capable of creating and how we can adapt to change by being resourceful." He is not alone in that belief: In a 2010 IBM poll of CEOs worldwide, creativity was identified as the single most important leadership trait for success, enabling businesses and workers to rise above an increasingly complex environment. The future belongs to "creators and empathizers, pattern recognizers and meaning makers," declared author Daniel Pink in his bestselling book *A Whole New Mind: Why Right-Brainers Will Rule the Future.*

There is, perhaps, no more compelling story of how imagination can save a person's life than Viktor Frankl's life under the Nazi regime. Frankl was a psychiatrist who spent three years during World War II living under unspeakable circumstances in several Nazi concentration camps. While imprisoned, Frankl realized he had one single freedom left: the power to determine his response to the horror unfolding around him. And so he chose to imagine. He imagined his wife and the prospect of seeing her again. He imagined himself after the war, teaching students about the lessons he had learned in the camps.

Frankl survived and went on to chronicle his experiences and the wisdom he had drawn from them. "A human being is a deciding being," he wrote in his 1946 book, *Man's Search for Meaning.* "Everything can be taken from a man but one thing: the last of the human freedoms—to choose one's attitude in any given set of circumstances, to choose one's own way." It is exactly that "power to choose our response" that underscores the importance of creativity.

The author Deepak Chopra beautifully describes an expansive creativity as a manifestation of abundance, a representation of the spiritual law of pure potentiality. He explains that we are, in our essential state, pure consciousness—a potentiality that represents the field of all possibilities and infinite creativity. Only when we discover this essential nature in ourselves and become aware of who we are at our core can we fully realize the ability to fulfill our dreams. Because we represent an eternal possibility, "the immeasurable potential of all that was, is and will be."[57]

The Creativity Bias

From an evolutionary standpoint, uncertainty was a bad thing. If you weren't sure there was a predator in front of you, by the time you were sure, it was probably too late. Our brains thus evolved to take uncertainty and make it certain.[58] In recent times, we have approached the goal of creating certainty in our environment with a pathological sort of obsession, which manifests itself in virtually every aspect of our lives. (Recall Jill Bolte Taylor's description of the left brain as the master of details, details and more details about those details.) This obsessive quest for certainty adversely impacts a trait that is key to resilience: creativity.

Creativity suffers from an odd sort of paradox. Psychologist and Wharton professor Jennifer Mueller studies creativity. Her research shows that even as people explicitly aspire to be creative and strongly endorse creativity as a fundamental driving force of positive change, they routinely reject creative ideas in their daily lives and show an implicit bias against them under conditions of uncertainty. Subjects in Mueller's study exhibited a failure to see or acknowledge creativity, even when directly presented with it.

The phenomenon is identified by Mueller as the "creativity bias." Even though most of us suffer from this bias, we are also

---

[57] Deepak Chopra, *The Seven Spiritual Laws of Success.*

[58] Beau Lotto.

in denial about it, since there is a strong social drive to endorse creativity. People feel such highly positive attitudes toward creativity that they are reluctant to admit that they do not necessarily wish to be creative themselves. And this is why Mueller finds the bias against creativity may be slippery to diagnose.

In her research, Mueller has found that innovation and change are, at their very essence, a "why" proposition. The "how" comes later. It is in this way that perception often becomes the gateway to change. People are so averse to uncertainty that they can't see creativity. They are blind to it. But by becoming aware of our mindsets and perceptions, we can step in the direction of breakthroughs.

Our wise artist and neuroscientist Beau Lotto calls "why" the most dangerous word in history. Because the creation of all new perceptions begins in the same way—with a single question: "Why?" As soon as you ask that question, you open up the possibility of change. So asking "why" may be the hardest thing for people to do.

Jennifer Mueller's research also showed a perceived dissonance between creativity and practicality—the "why" people and the "how" people, in her terminology. People focused on "why" tend to frame the world in more abstract ways and are concerned less with practical questions. Those in a "how" mindset may be so focused on practical questions that they are likely to overlook or dismiss creative ideas.

"Most boardrooms are all 'how,' and the 'why' is crushed," Mueller says. "This is why Steve Jobs was so remarkable. He had a solid grasp of the 'why' and was also able to overcome objections to the 'how.' He was able to overcome the reality distortion field."

The shortcomings of Mueller's "how" people were on full display in the 2008 financial collapse. In a fascinating study of mindset among bankers, New America Foundation senior fellow and founder of the Better Banking Project Susan Ochs discovered an overwhelming trend toward a fixed mindset averse to uncertainty among the bankers.[59] The top mental model among the industry professionals revealed their belief that complex solutions are not just necessary, but also a sign of high intelligence. Another prevalent theme among bankers: "I am rarely caught by surprise," indicating their confidence in the ability to control and even eliminate all uncertainty. We as a society have all paid the price for that delusion.

The most troubling of Ochs's findings is that the mindsets among the bankers remain largely unchanged since before the financial crisis.

Another reason for the bias against creativity may be the perception that something can be either creative or practical, but rarely both. So we have a bias toward duality, where practical and creative endeavors lead largely separate existences—one slogged at during the workweek and the other indulged on nights and weekends, if not dismissed as a luxury.

So here lies the dilemma: Creativity is what we need to help us get through times of greatest uncertainty and difficulty. And it's exactly during those times—perhaps when we need it most—that we are least likely to embrace creativity. Imagination scares us because it demands a foray into the unknown. But only by venturing into that realm of the unknown can we do anything new. It is a tremendous challenge, isn't it?

Think of all the tools created to make life predictable—from packaged foods to Starbucks, GPS devices to smartphones, Yelp to TripAdvisor. The problem is that the more we seek to create

---

[59] Susan M. Ochs, "Inside the Banker's Brain: Mental Models in the Financial Services Industry and Implications for Consumers, Practitioners and Regulators," Aspen Institute, June 2014.

tools to make life predictable, the more we diminish aspects of our brains capable of dealing with the unexpected. Technology is an amazing tool and yet a huge impairment to our capacity for resilience and handling uncertain, potentially stressful circumstances.[60]

And the interesting wrinkle to our never-ending quest for certainty is that it does not exist.

"Certainty is an illusion! A delusion!" says neuroscientist Beau Lotto. It all comes down to the subjectivity of our perceptions.

◆   ◆   ◆

Is it possible to overcome our inclination toward the predictable? Yes. There are practical ways to start on the path to growth and innovation.

Professor Mueller's research highlights an important exception to our avoidance of the unknown. The way we frame uncertainty can change the way people react to it. As it turns out, we don't mind uncertainty when it's associated with something positive, like hope. If you frame something positively, people will behave differently toward it. You must, at the outset, be certain that you want change, says Mueller. "You must be clear strategically whether you really are looking for something groundbreaking. Define what that means. Sometimes people call something innovation, but it really isn't."

David Kelley seeks to democratize creativity by helping people develop creative confidence. Creativity involves being comfortable with your ideas and being willing to put those ideas out there. We are not teaching people how to be creative, because they are inherently creative. "All we are doing is taking away the blocks, which form early," Kelley observes. Though young chil-

---

[60] Laura Richardson, principal designer, Frog Design.

dren are naturally and unabashedly creative, they often lose confidence as they grow older or have it hammered out of them in elementary school. "A kind of atrophy sets in when they start to trust their analytical minds, but not their intuitive minds."

Creative confidence means chipping away at those long-standing, hardened blocks. Kelley believes that creative blocks have a great deal to do with fear and recommends approaching the fear of creativity the same way you would approach any other fear. Creative confidence impacts our perceptions and our stories about ourselves. It carries over into other aspects of our lives—in the way we solve problems, sing karaoke, throw dinner parties and deal with potentially stressful situations. Once you have done something you fear and succeed, you are emboldened in other contexts. And you begin to learn how to synthesize your experience and intuition to make complex and important decisions to gain a mastery over challenges, big and small.

The Power to Choose a Response

The underlying aim of Lotto's research is to help people transform by enabling them to understand and become part of learning about their own perceptions. His hope is that people will walk away from his experiments not with an understanding of color or shape, but with an understanding of themselves, or at least a question of themselves.

The first step, however, is through awareness. Self-awareness. Consciousness.

You must see yourself see, says Lotto. It's about observation and curiosity, having a sense of wonder, becoming aware of the connection between the past and the present. Becoming an observer of yourself enables you to do amazing things.

In the end, what we are fighting for is our imagination—the right to imagine a life and relationships and a social world that is happier, less anxious, more harmonious and more just. As Princeton professor Ruha Benjamin observed: "We are not being diligent enough or deliberate enough about cultivating our imagination. We have to fight for our ability to imagine the world we want. Because one form of oppression is telling people that they're not allowed to imagine something better and happier."

Practice

- **Be conscious of habits.**
  Professor Benjamin says: "Become aware of how your habitat forms your habits." Consider the ways you can apply this insight to your life. Take any perception you find questionable and do your best to remain conscious of it for an entire week. Write down your thoughts about your experience and how your awareness changed (or did not change).

- **Find and embrace your creativity.**
  Quickly and without thinking about it too much, name the top three ways you think you are creative. With those answers in mind, ask yourself this question: What if my life depended on my ability to be creative? Now ask yourself: What are the top three ways my ability to create might save my life?

Rule 4

Be Free

The mind is everything. What you think, you become.

—BUDDHA

It's being called a "late bloomer" that irks Shilloy Sanchez the most.

In the early 2000s Shilloy Sanchez was living in New York City with her young daughter. She was rising up in a blue-chip marketing firm. And as far as she could tell, she was on track for the American dream. "Not early, not late, but on track," she says. "I was keeping up with the Joneses, with the education, the salary, the home, aiming for the 2.5 kids by a certain age.

"For decades I had been going through the motions of what you should be doing when you're successful," she recalls. "Maybe my work was still not answering the question of who I was, but I justified it as, 'I'll make all the money I want to make and then I'll do what I really want to do.'"

In 2006 Shilloy moved to the West Coast and was recruited by a technology start-up. Within three years, the company went bust, along with the economy. What followed was the most stressful period of her life, marked by deep despair.

"I cried and prayed. And I grieved. I mourned the person I

thought I was going to be. I mourned the company that I thought was going to take off. I mourned my home, my car, all the material things I was surrounded by that, in the end, had nothing to do with my comfort, my happiness or my salvation."

With her savings spent, she packed up her home and placed everything in storage. And she did what had once seemed unthinkable to her: She moved back to her parents' house. She needed to take some time to think about what was happening.

Within months, she identified that missing thing that had eluded her all those decades.

What she was meant to do—go back to school to become a therapist—fell into place. There had always been an inkling of it in her life, but she had never slowed down to contemplate the possibility. She was driven by all the other things she thought she was supposed to do and so she made a series of unconscious decisions over the course of years. Eventually the unconscious living shaped her life.

But once disaster struck, she was forced to stop and look around. It was only then that the path became clear. And then it was just a matter of simple details: which school, which program, which classes.

"I was having one of those magical moments," she told me. "It was smooth like it was meant to be. As if the script had been written and I was finally willing to read it. It felt right and good."

Shilloy recalls putting pen to paper one morning during those four months of disquiet at her parents' home. She wrote a simple question: "What do I want?"

The answer she scribbled down that day still hangs nearby: "A life where I am present. A life where I serve. A life where I don't resent others. A life that allows me the chance to make a difference. A life that is extraordinary. A life where I laugh often. A life full of love."

One year later, almost to the day, Shilloy's dreams became her reality. Today she is a therapist specializing in eating disorders. "If that is what's called being a late bloomer," she told me, "so be it. But I don't know that I could have gotten here any earlier without going through everything I went through. I couldn't even imagine it before." She had been too busy playing the roles she thought she was supposed to play.

At first she was broken. And then she broke free. Working harder than she ever had. Living differently than she had ever expected. And happier than she had ever been.

"The thing that has become most important to me is my connection to my purpose. People constantly say to me, 'I wish I could do what you're doing.' And I think to myself: 'You could.'"

Perhaps Shilloy is not a late bloomer, but she has become, at the very least, a woman in full bloom.

•   •   •

The principle of inertia as described by Isaac Newton in his First Law of Motion holds that an object will always continue moving at its current speed, and in its current direction, unless acted upon by some outside force.

Oprah Winfrey once expressed the principle in a slightly different way:

> I say the universe speaks to us, always, first in
>   whispers . . .
> And if you don't pay attention to the whisper, it gets
>   louder and louder and louder.
> I say it's like getting thumped upside the head.
> If you don't pay attention to that, it's like getting a
>   brick upside your head.

> You don't pay attention to that—the brick wall falls
> down.
> This is the pattern I see in my life and so many other
> people's lives.[61]

I know that I have looked back at the events of my own life and wondered which was the whisper, which the thump and which the brick. I can take a pretty good guess at what the brick wall was.

Precisely as Mr. Newton predicted, I changed both in direction and speed.

Are the calamities that change the course of our lives from one direction to another constructive stress or destructive stress? It depends on our response.

Our values are often held by default. Sometimes we sleepwalk through life, stuck in stasis surrounding our jobs, our environments, our relationships, even our self-identity. In a very fundamental sense, stress is about the resistance that comes about when our static definitions about life and lifestyles are threatened, and we don't feel free to change.

Sometimes stressful life circumstances themselves can lead to change. We view these disruptions as calamities, but often they are the quakes that force our hand to tap into unknown potential, *forcing* a bloom, thereby becoming the calamity that creates providence. It is these calamities that give us no choice, but to "free" ourselves from rote scripts, habits and expectations.

Being free is closely related to creativity and there is some overlap, to be sure. But if *creativity* is the ability to take risks, to imagine, to play, to dare to engage in our deepest passions and

---

[61] Oprah Winfrey, Master Class: http://www.oprah.com/own-master-class/Oprah-Winfreys-Master-Class-Quotes.

sometimes fail at them, *freedom* is the power to extend our individual boundaries as far as possible. It's about defining our own boundaries. And ultimately, being free involves daring to stretch to take up the entirety of the space we have each been allotted, as opposed to cowering, cramped, in one corner.

Unactualized Potential

Few of us know what we are truly capable of when pushed. Author David Shenk writes that "the vast majority of us have not even come close to tapping what scientists call our 'unactualized potential.' "[62] This is in large part because we've become so stuck in the narrative we've created for ourselves. Being free is part creativity, part storytelling, part brazen audacity—and in no small measure, fear of that brick wall.

And for many, it involves an examination of our beliefs about early bloomers, and about success, genius and destiny.

Cognitive psychologist Scott Barry Kaufman points out that there is only one way to become an early bloomer but, in contrast, an infinite number of ways to become a late bloomer. There are no predetermined paths to greatness, he observes, only paths that have already come and those that have yet to come.

While we as a society are fascinated by younger people who show precocious, rapid development in comparison with their peers, those early bloomers very rarely go on to become trendsetters or innovators. Late bloomers' achievements, on the other hand, can be far-reaching because they tend to require quite complex abilities that are often years in the making—even if this scenario lacks that allure of the wunderkind.

---

[62] David Shenk, *The Genius in All of Us*.

The Myths of Aging

The past decade has been a difficult time for many, especially for the unemployed, broken down psychologically, economically, socially and physically. Though there are rarely any easy answers, sometimes the simple act of freeing ourselves from both conscious and unconscious social narratives we buy into—whether a certain social class, type of employment or geographical region— illuminates a new path. This freedom can liberate us from the clutches of destructive stress. Being flexible, open and "free" is a gateway to reframing stressful circumstances on many levels. And at no time is this more important—or difficult—as in the later stages of life.

Debra Dunn, an associate professor at the Stanford Institute of Design, was a senior executive at Hewlett-Packard for twenty-two years. Steeped in Silicon Valley culture, she recalls that some of the most wonderfully innovative engineers she knew were old-timers. Ultimately, though, she observes that older people's perceptions of their own ability to contribute became powerful predictors of what they could and could not achieve.

Our culture notoriously celebrates youth. Look around and you will find both subtle and not so subtle means of belittling women and men who fear aging, fighting the passing of years by any means necessary. But what appears at first glance to be vanity is often much more complex than that. Sometimes it's not getting older that people object to as much as the dread of the loss of opportunities. And diving deeper, we find that the loss of opportunities, too, is for the most part just a perception—a kind of prison imposed by both oneself and society.

There are many myths of growing older that help feed our perceptions of being stuck. Google "the aging brain" and you will find a largely sobering landscape of cognitive deterioration. But turn the kaleidoscope of our knowledge about the aging brain and a far more interesting picture emerges.

The prevailing wisdom is that creative endeavors are good for helping to slow the decline of our mental capabilities. But what if, in fact, the aging brain is more capable than its younger counterpart of creativity and innovation?

It's a compelling proposition in our society. More and more seniors are looking for jobs and going back to work—the number of working seniors has more than doubled since 1990, according to the Bureau of Labor Statistics. Ageism is rampant in many areas, particularly in hiring. And innovation is, for the most part, considered a young person's domain.

A large body of research about aging tells us that as we cross the threshold into middle age, neural connections that receive, process and transmit information can weaken from age and disuse. It may take us longer to learn new information. We often can't think as sharply or as quickly. Our reaction times may be slower.

Researchers also tell us that older people have a harder time multitasking. We can become more forgetful, resulting in those tip-of-the-tongue moments where familiar words, names and concepts lie just out of reach. An older person is more easily distracted and more prone to daydreaming and errors. ("Funny," said the dashing older gentleman. "I don't remember being absentminded.")

All this may seem disconcerting, but it is also an incomplete picture. In his book *Major Issues in Cognitive Aging*, Timothy A. Salthouse, professor of psychology and director of the Cognitive Aging Laboratory at the University of Virginia, writes, "Although there is no shortage of opinions about cognitive aging, it sometimes seems that relatively few of the claims are based on well-established empirical evidence. . . . Assertions about cognitive aging may be influenced as much by the authors' preconceptions and attitudes as by systematic evaluations of empirical research." Salthouse goes on to make two more significant observations about cognitive aging: Discoveries of decline in the laboratory do not necessarily correlate to success out in the real world, and there is often considerable variation among different people of the same age.

Place these findings alongside research about the power of suggestion, where the anticipation and expectations of a specific outcome drive subsequent thoughts and behaviors that can actually bring the expected outcome to fruition. And suddenly you have a whole new narrative about the possibilities of healthy aging.[63]

Research details a number of ways in which the brain actually improves with age. And many of these advanced abilities correlate with innovation, creativity and the foundations of "design thinking"—a human-centered method for creative problem solving, as outlined by the Institute of Design at Stanford.[64] The pillars of the design thinking process—the ability to empathize, define, ideate, prototype and test—correlate with characteristics of healthy aging, revealing clearly how neurocircuitry factors can favor age in terms of innovation.

The foundation of a human-centered design process is empathy, which is critical to understanding the people for whom you are designing. Older people have a greater capacity for empathy because empathy is learned and refined as we age.

---

[63] One of my favorite comments to my piece "A Creative Life Is a Healthy Life" was by one of the readers, Ron, who wrote: "Want REAL innovation? Bring in the seniors."

[64] In broad terms, human-centered design is a type of design process built around needs, wants and limitations of the people using the product. Because of this, empathy with the potential user becomes a key component of the design process.

"How many adolescents do you know with the gift of empathy?" asks Kathleen Taylor, a professor at St. Mary's College of California and an internationally recognized authority on adult learning. Not many, as it turns out. Coming up short on empathy characterizes our teen years and continues into the twenties—and much longer for some. According to Taylor, younger people are more likely to connect with others from their own place of need. A twenty-two-year-old may have an idea, and that idea may be quite brilliant and useful, but more than likely it'll be all tied up in the narrow egocentric perspective of that one young person. Because of their greater capacity to empathize, older people tend to have a far wider perspective and broader understanding about others' needs and desires.

Older people are also highly capable when it comes to the "define" aspect of human-centered design—that is, the unpacking and synthesizing of empathy findings into compelling needs and insights. A riper brain can better tease out patterns and see the big picture. Whereas younger people may have better short-term and get-to-the-point-quickly memory, older folks have had a greater variety of experiences and are better able to build a wider image out of a lot of different parts. They can make more connections because they have so much more to bring to bear on their current pursuits.[65]

Put another way by design legend Steve Jobs in an interview with *Wired* in the 1990s: "A lot of people in our industry haven't had very diverse experiences. So they don't have enough dots to connect, and they end up with very linear solutions without a broad perspective on the problem. The broader one's understanding of the human experience, the better design we will have." Of course, seniors "can sometimes lose those dots," Taylor notes

---

[65] Gary Small, professor of psychiatry and director of the UCLA Center on Aging.

with a smile. "But only temporarily, because remember: We absolutely never reach the full capacity of our brain."

Which brings us back to unactualized potential.

As we get older, so much more is stored in our brain—it's like having overfull drawers. And those things you can't quite recall? They haven't disappeared. They're just tucked away in the folds of your neurons. You can't necessarily find everything in it, but it's all still there.

As we age, we are better able to anticipate problems and reason things out than when we were young. Research shows that our complex reasoning skills continue to improve as we get older. But this capacity can also serve as a double-edged sword.

Albert Einstein famously said that we can't solve problems through the same kind of thinking as when we created them. As we age, yesterday's thinking can form an invisible box that some may resist venturing out of today. The advantage young people have is that they don't try to solve problems with yesterday's solutions—mainly because they aren't even aware of those solutions and are thus unencumbered by them. Often, young people have no clue about the places where they shouldn't be treading, says Taylor. "And ultimately, they go outside the box because they don't know there is a box."[66]

There's a certain fearlessness to ignorance. But balance fearlessness against wisdom, which can guide the aging brain to greater insights that will advance creativity and innovation. Here, once again, mindfulness enters the picture. Professor Gary Small, director of the UCLA Center on Aging, emphasizes the importance of mindfulness by pointing out that, as he gets older, he thinks more in terms of what is meaningful in his life right now rather than what he can do to make things better in the future.

---

[66] Dr. Kathleen Taylor.

Maybe it's because you realize that your horizon is less far off, he says, so you tend to live more in the present. That contributes to creativity. You are able to notice more about yourself and others in your environment, leading to new ideas that can be incredibly useful.

Small's work at UCLA shows clearly that the older brain is magnificently resilient and can be stimulated to innovate, create and contribute in extraordinary ways. Much of cognitive impairment is due to the decline in creativity that can result from people's capabilities not being challenged, Small suggests. He offers his own profession as a university professor as an example: "You go from researching, writing and coming up with new ideas to becoming a manager and department dean, where you're basically writing speeches and managing people and institutions, which does not really bring out a whole lot of creative energy." He would like to see incentives to encourage older people to continue to be creative because what they have to offer is tremendous.

The Path to Freedom

I interviewed Tony Wagner, Expert in Residence at Harvard's new Innovation Lab, soon after he published his compelling book, *Creating Innovators*. We discussed how people well past what our culture defines as their prime can expand their perceptions and stories. The path to innovation is still there as we get older, observes Wagner, but it can become more difficult to find later in life, in part because of the inertia. We must work very hard to listen to ourselves, because the distractions continue to multiply. And here is where imagination and creativity become key to the process.

Living a life of innovation needs no justification, but there are plenty of good reasons—both pragmatic and otherwise—to do so.

Innovating, imagining and creating give us a sense of purpose, Wagner says. If you lack those things, or if you get stuck on repeat, a pervasive sense of emptiness becomes the default. And then people resort to drastic—and not always healthy—measures to fill the void.

The first question Wagner asks of older innovators is the biggest one: Are you willing to settle for less money? In the course of his work, Wagner has met dozens of professionals who have managed to cut loose. He recalled one woman trained as an MD who was teaching high school science. She settled for far less money, but was much happier.

More questions Wagner suggested asking yourself: Am I giving back? Am I making a difference? Am I following my passion when I'm not working, or has working become an addiction?

Do these questions sound familiar? They are very similar to the ones Shilloy Sanchez asked herself at her moment of greatest despair. She turned what she first saw as a devastating loss into a magnificent new start, and in the process freed herself from long-held assumptions, fears and expectations.

As Shilloy learned, it is never too late to find your path in life. But in order to find that path, we must first free our minds from the bogus script of how our lives "should be." This is the greatest freedom.

Practice

Freeing ourselves from long-held and deeply entrenched stories is a formidable task and the path to innovation can be an unconventional one. Wagner offers advice to help guide the way:

- **Shut out the noise.**
  At some point it's time to stop blaming family, friends and life circumstances, and to look inward. Ultimately the path to innovation requires a certain kind of inner strength, a spiritual discipline. It's important to cultivate the discipline of listening to yourself. Even if you have no support, the support that ultimately matters most must come from within you.

- **Believe in yourself and your vision.**
  Begin by making a declaration of yourself and your intentions. Put a stake in the ground by making a statement out loud in front of a mirror. Write about your passions in a journal. We all have ideas, but you can't follow your dream or vision unless you can give it a voice.

- **Continue to learn.**
  We are wired to be lifelong learners. It's in our DNA. Is the spirit of curiosity still alive as you get older? Do you listen to your own questions, ideas and interests? Do you make time for them? Continue to study things that you care about and develop an area of expertise, inside or outside a formal classroom setting. Seek out teachers who are passionate about their subjects. Make a sustained effort over time to master your own interests.

- **Redefine failure and embrace iteration.**
  By now, you surely have failed—probably more than you'd like. If you haven't, you must be playing it too safe. Accept failure! Even though it "hurts like hell—especially failing in public . . . you will learn some of your most valuable lessons from failure—far more than from your successes. We need to redefine 'failure' as a society. It has become a pejorative in our vocabulary," says Wagner. No one wants to fail, and yet you can't pursue passion and purpose without a great deal of trial and error. And this involves multiple failures. Wagner prefers the term "iteration," a design concept that involves the continuous prototyping, testing, analyzing and refining of an idea or product.

- **Have fun.**
  Creativity, imagination and innovation usually find us during moments of play. Take time off and find ways to recharge your creative and physical energy. Take walks, get regular exercise, spend time in nature, listen to music, study paintings and photographs, volunteer.

- **Exit the echo chamber.**
  Practice listening to many different kinds of people and ideas. More people are choosing their sources of news by listening only to those who reinforce their biases and points of view. This does you a disservice. Experience other cultures. Read a thoughtful opinion piece that is diametrically opposed to your own. Read history and good novels. Explore other religions as a way of understanding the world.
  Travel is important as a way of expanding our view and upsetting our inclination toward equilibrium. But the type of travel matters. Are you engaging in just another form of consumption or undertaking a potentially life-changing learning

experience? Do you immerse yourself in authentic experiences or wall yourself off in a cocoon of the familiar? Travel with the purpose of really understanding a culture, a way of life and being that is radically different from your own.

- **Work hard at mastery.**
  By now, you are probably no stranger to discipline and hard work. In his book *Outliers*, Malcolm Gladwell writes about the importance of putting in ten thousand hours to master something. There are no shortcuts to mastery for anyone—young or old. Remember: Genius is 1 percent inspiration and 99 percent perspiration, in the wise words of Thomas Edison.

- **Engage in self-reflection.**
  Wagner emphasizes the importance of establishing a regular mindfulness practice through writing in a journal, walking, yoga or other pursuits.

CHAPTER SEVEN

Your Mind

"What do you miss most about Brazil?"

"I'm not sure how to say in English. Can I e-mail you?"

"Just try."

"In Brazil. My people. Money or no money. Still happy."

—*Humans of New York*

Rule 5

Be Happy

The day started out for John Russo the same as every other day. He arrived at his corner office on the third floor of his company's Silicon Valley building at eight a.m. He closed his door so he could prepare for the day. His assistant, stationed just outside the door, was tasked with keeping everyone out for the first half hour, but with a few hundred people in his department—many of them eager to catch him as quickly as possible, usually on a budget issue—that was not easy to do. On this particular day, he logged on to his laptop and saw that he had more than 150 new e-mails. He looked up and he could see, from the corner of his eye, that several directors who reported to him kept dropping by. "Is he available?" he heard being asked over and over again. He turned away from the door and glanced out the window. That's when he saw the line at the Starbucks that sat catty-corner from his office. The line forming out the door was thirty to forty people deep. His chest tightened at the sight. He was trying to focus on his schedule, but he kept glancing at the people in the Starbucks line, inching forward, waiting to grab their coffee. And a single thought kept bubbling up: *What am I doing here?*

The mantra of John's tech company was: "We are going to change the world." The CEO would initiate new hires by putting a temporary tattoo on their foreheads, effectively branding them with the company's logo. The execs would talk among themselves about how to get people to adopt the belief that they were creating a life-altering product. "We were making a billing system that charged money for people using their cell phones," John says with a chuckle. But people bought into it lock, stock, and barrel. He remembers employees—many of them with young families—working long hours, sometimes all night.

For some weeks John had also been stressing over a health issue. One day he wondered what his obituary might say if something bad happened. "All I could come up with was: 'John Russo worked in Silicon Valley for thirty-three years. He worked all day and often most of the night. He made a billing system.'" This thought depressed him to no end.

On that day, gazing out the window, Russo said to himself: "I've got to get out of this place. I am more than this. Humans are more than this."

Earlier that year John had bought a small farm a few hours away and he started taking his family down on the weekends. The only thing he could remember was how quiet it was. He would arrive late on a Friday night and go sit outside alone, trying to unwind. "But all I could hear was ringing in my ears. Saturday, I would hear the ringing all day. On Sunday, the ringing would subside and then stop. Then I would get on the road by two o'clock to beat the traffic back."

For the first time in his life, John started plotting his exit. It was not so easy. "I used to visualize it as a gravitational pull," he says. But he was a vice president and he couldn't just leave. From the day he told his boss, it took him almost eight months to actually get out the door. Although the execs were all ultimately disposable, management didn't want John to just disappear. John had been at the company for five years. He was well liked and there was concern that his departure might affect morale. They told him to keep it a secret, asked him to stick around, to ease out gradually. "Like the Mafia, the cult didn't allow quitting," John jokes.

His resignation was seen as an insult. Some months later, when he asked for a letter of recommendation, he was refused. "The person I asked told me he hadn't really known me that well. Five years I worked there."

This, he says, was one of the most important lessons he learned after quitting: that most of his important relationships had only been part of the business. After that context was gone, there was nothing left. Most of the people who saw him every day—whom he had considered friends—barely stayed in touch after he left.

No wonder so many people who lose their jobs fall into depression, he says. "Everyone has a human worth, but in the corporate world we called people 'resources,' and now you even call them capital. But capital is a possession. A human possessed. It's actually woven into the way you view the people and it defines the relationship. If you are working twelve hours a day, those relationships are your life. And then one day, when the sales are not met, your whole life is gone."

John Russo was lost for a period. He had spent his whole life in high tech and he had no idea what he was going to do. He wanted to move to his farm, but his wife refused. So they moved south, to a small town, closer to the farm.

Soon he began working on another high-tech venture. "It's funny," he admits, "how you end up doing the same thing over and over again." He completed a successful pilot on the new product and began gearing up to talk to venture capitalists.

Then there was an accident, a fire that burned down his new house. No one was hurt, but it was a disaster—an incredibly stressful period. Later, he would see the disaster differently. He would see it as serendipity.

After the fire, he and his family were living in a hotel room, trying to find a place to rent, when a couple asked to rent his farm while they did some work on their property nearby.

Why not? John thought. He hadn't stepped foot on the farm in months. He went to check the place out, clean it up a bit so he could show it.

The place was an absolute mess. The deer had eaten all the landscaping. The garden's water system had broken, and almost everything that the deer hadn't consumed had died in a drought. John began the difficult task of trying to clean up and get the place back into shape.

As he walked back and forth on the main path that day, one giant bush—the only flora still alive—kept hitting him the face. Annoyed, he went to get the hedge trimmer and started hacking at the plant. He almost felt as if he were in a trance, clipping, cutting. So intent was John on his task that it took him a minute or two to notice that he was standing in a cloud of fragrance. The scent was overwhelming, heavenly. It snapped him into the present, into his surroundings. Everything dead and dry all around him, looking horrible. Except for this giant plant that had flourished in spite of it all. There it stood, obstinately in the way, as if to say: Pick me! Pick me!

This plant! he thought. *There must be something that can be done with this plant.*

The pesky plant was a Grosso lavender.

He finished up at the farm and rented the place. Then he began researching what he could do with the lavender. He visited farms up and down the coast, from San Diego to Seattle. As he traveled, he envisioned an integrated life of family and work, intertwined, in harmony. "I thought about all that stuff I could have never done in the corporate world, where if you ever bring your family to work, they treat you as if you have a third head. You can just see the disdain in their eyes."

John's old house in Los Altos had a pool, but he never actually used it. One day he arrived home early. He drove up and found the gardener sitting knee-deep in the flower beds by the pool, working and whistling, thoroughly enjoying the beautiful day. On that day, John wished, wistfully, that he could sit there like the gardener and do what he did.

And now a plan began to take shape for John Russo. Perhaps, he thought, it wasn't such a crazy idea after all. Within one year, Russo would establish his farm and company, Carmel Lavender.

♦ ♦ ♦

For a period of years, I considered myself one of the most miserable lawyers to walk the earth. This is no easy feat, since at any given time there are multitudes of miserable lawyers walking the earth. But I was singularly, deliriously unhappy, and though I made a decent enough salary during my years of misery, I spent most of my money trying to forget how unhappy I was.

Studies show that the stress of work is consuming many of us. Confucius said that if you choose a job you love, you will never work a day in your life. Confucius must have known then what science now confirms: Passion and purpose protect us physiologically, allowing us to work longer and harder than we would if toiling away at a job we hate.

Ask people what they want out of life and there is a good chance they will tell you they just want to be happy. Follow up by asking what exactly that means and you are likely to stump them. It is one of life's great ironies that most of us can barely say what "being happy" really means. I had an intuition that I was in the wrong profession for years before I did anything about it. I had many reasons. Three years of law school and tens of thousands of dollars in student loans had vested me in being a lawyer. I had doubled down with a postgraduate degree in law. There was a huge amount of pressure from my family to remain a lawyer. And on and on. In the end, though, I made my exit and I never looked back. All I wanted was to be happy.

Tomes have been written about happiness, most in an attempt to pin down what is acknowledged to be an exercise in futility, "a slippery concept, a bundle of meanings with no precise, stable definition."[67] There is nothing inherently wrong with this uncertainty, since happiness is best experienced as a lifelong adventure with its ebbs and flows. The problems arise when the elusive reality of happiness bumps up against our need for a more immediate and clear-cut gratification.

There is a great deal of pressure in our culture to "be happy." Happiness is fundamental to our sense of self and success. Even the American Declaration of Independence lists happiness as an inalienable right—third, after only life and liberty. We live in a world filled with messages about how to "acquire" happiness, whether through material goods or other means.

Our relentless, almost culturally mandated pursuit of happiness lies at the core of a great deal of confusion and misunderstanding which, in turn, contributes to behaviors that create cycles of great stress in our lives. And when the dogged pursuit of the material becomes an end rather than the means, we effectively become trapped in that surreal space where you can be simultaneously "happy," desperately dissatisfied and chronically stressed. Was this, ultimately, what John Russo and I were feeling in our respective professional lives?

To address this all too familiar and destructive stress—and to untangle the mystery of true happiness—we need a better understanding and greater consciousness of the motivations that drive us in our daily lives. And we need to redirect those motiva-

---

[67] Eduardo Porter, *The Price of Everything*.

tions toward a different set of goals—goals that are aligned with our true purpose and give our lives a sense of meaning.

This process of discovery is difficult. It requires the kind of self-reflection and commitment to reality that many people are reluctant to undertake because, well, it involves a bit of sacrifice and suffering and these can be stressful. It's the Catch-22 of happiness: You are going to experience stress either way. But it is imperative that you experience the *right* sort of stress, constructive stress, the kind we must learn to become comfortable with and even welcome into our lives.

The most important distinction to be made here is between the suffering necessary to find true happiness and the suffering caused by our pursuit of false proxies for happiness. The former, what psychologist M. Scott Peck calls "legitimate suffering" in *The Road Less Traveled*, is needed for growth, whereas the latter is caused by avoidance. People attempt to go over and go under legitimate suffering, and in so doing they end up suffering even more. "Neurosis," observed Carl Jung, "is always a substitute for legitimate suffering."

"Happiness is when what you think, what you say and what you do are in harmony," wrote Mahatma Gandhi. Our inquiry into the equation of true happiness mirrors this definition. First, we must first determine what we value most. Next, what is actually motivating us? And finally, a hard reckoning of the extent to which these two are in alignment with our day-to-day actions: herein lies the disconnect at the root of a world of destructive stress.

■ **What are your values?**
Our true beliefs and values form the foundation upon which we build our lives. Identifying, defining and expressly listing these values are critical parts of our quest.

- **What are your motivations?**

Our motivations tend to be a mix of the intrinsic and the extrinsic. Intrinsic goals are often rooted in altruism, correlating with the foundations of a life of character and spiritual pursuits. They can be centered on family, friends, achievements, social commitments and relevance to family and society and, as such, are more emotionally rewarding. They demand that we examine and work on personal growth, self-knowledge and self-awareness. They urge us toward better connections with others and greater social intimacy. Through intrinsic motivations we consider how we might serve and advance community, society, humanity and faith. Research—and common sense—reveals that people view intrinsic goals as the most important and meaningful.

Extrinsic goals represent the other end of the spectrum of motivations. They skew toward more materialistic aspirations, like appearances, money and fame; more broadly, they may involve the quest for power, status and popularity, as well as attractiveness and luxury.[68] The dilemma of a singular focus on extrinsic goals becomes even more tightly knotted when these key outer markers become the metrics by which we measure success, accomplishment and self-esteem. And with that comes the striving, the competition, the endless hours of work, the neglect of friends, family and faith.[69] It will come as no surprise that extrinsic values often correlate with narcissism, self-absorption and egotism, leading to an even greater emphasis on the dogged pursuit of material pursuits. It creates a tsunami of destructive stress and anxiety, from which we are led to believe there is no escape. In short, it's a formula for disaster.

---

[68] Research by Kennon M. Sheldon, quoted in Philip Moeller, "Why Seeking More Money Hurts Happiness," *U.S. News & World Report*, April 9, 2012.

[69] Jean Twenge interview. Also see Moeller, "Why Seeking More Money Hurts Happiness."

When I announced I was leaving my first law firm, another young attorney came into my office to congratulate me. "You are so lucky to be going," he said, his face wistful. "I wish it could be me, too."

"Why couldn't it be you?" I asked.

"The house, the mortgage, the car, the schools, the bills," he said. "You know, the golden collar."

By and large, we are, as a society, convinced that we are tethered by the golden collar, that we have no choice but to embrace extrinsic values because that's the way the world operates and that's what we must do to "play the game" and remain competitive.

That's not to say there is no relationship between money and well-being.

"More money does not necessarily buy more happiness," writes Nobel Prize–winning psychologist Daniel Kahneman. "But less money is associated with emotional pain." In an extensive study involving health and well-being data collected from almost half a million Americans, Kahneman and economist Angus Deaton found a measurable connection between income and happiness. Poverty and financial strain consistently top most stress surveys. People with more money have more comfortable lives than those living in poverty, and their higher incomes are associated with better moods on a daily basis.[70] Money buys us and our loved ones necessities, opportunities and adventures. It can also fund significant amounts of altruism and beneficial social impact, also correlated with less stress and greater life satisfaction.

Poverty is devastating. It is one of the foremost causes of toxic stress in our society. This is true for adults, of course, but it hits children especially hard. According to Harvard's Center on the Devel-

[70] According to British economist Andrew Oswald, evidence shows up in brain scans and in happiness equations, quoted in Moeller, "Why Seeking More Money Hurts Happiness."

oping Child, extreme poverty, along with neglect, abuse and severe maternal depression can wreak havoc on the young, weakening the architecture of their developing brains, "with long-term consequences for learning, behavior, and physical and mental health." People living in poverty evaluate their lives poorly and have a low sense of emotional well-being. Their misfortune is further exacerbated by loneliness, illness, broken families and many other factors.

People feel better about their lives as their incomes rise, but— here lies the major caveat—the beneficial effects of money taper off at the point where a person reaches a comfortable standard of living. Clearly, the number associated with a "comfortable standard" varies dramatically. In most of the United States, emotional well-being and happiness peak when incomes reach about $75,000 a year. Every time I quote this number to people who live in New York City, San Francisco or another city with an exorbitant cost of living, they shriek in protest.

Fair enough, but only up to a point. Kahneman's research is based on a huge national sample of more than four hundred thousand people. Clearly the cost of living varies profoundly from a small town in Virginia to Seattle to Palo Alto, and such variations do skew the median number. But the actual number is well beside the point—the deeper message transcends these differences. In terms of our actual day-to-day experiences, increases in income don't yield corresponding increases in happiness.[71] Kahneman found that once you're above that minimum threshold of comfort— whether it's $75,000 or twice that—the return in terms of happiness for each $1,000 increment is negligible.

So why work endless hours, sacrificing health, family and other

---

[71] Unpublished research by psychologist Elizabeth Dunn shows that money has a far stronger relationship to preventing sadness than it does to creating happiness. Elizabeth W. Dunn and Michael Norton, "Don't Indulge. Be Happy," *New York Times*, July 7, 2012.

priorities long after we have reached an income level that is enough to make us comfortable? Psychologist Elizabeth Dunn thinks most of us have an unrealistic expectation of how happy money can make us. In one study, for example, people thought if they doubled their income, they would be twice as happy. The reality was that those who did earn twice as much were less than 10 percent happier.[72]

The idea that success requires extreme self-focus that is ultimately rewarded by money, fame or other trappings is a myth, however. Even beyond growing unhappiness, there is a clear connection between extrinsic values and the physical effects of stress, including more headaches and stomachaches.

Children are not immune, either. Young people in extrinsically focused societies tend to experience the same stress symptoms as adults.[73] A study of more than nine million U.S. high school seniors and college freshmen revealed a steady increase in stress, mental health problems and related signs of unhappiness.[74] Psychologist Jean Twenge observes that this is particularly problematic for the younger generation. We are shaped by the totality of our experiences, she says. For older people, who have seen cultures come, go and evolve, these experiences are "averaged"—that is, new experiences are blended with the old. This "mutes" the impact of current culture. But for younger people, the prevailing norms are all they have ever known.[75]

Americans lead the globe in pursuits that correlate with extrinsic motivations. This path is validated by ever-present, glossy, alluring messages about the easy fast track to happiness. Re-

---

[72] Dunn and Norton, "Don't Indulge. Be Happy."

[73] Tim Kasser interview.

[74] Jean Twenge interview. Also see Moeller, "Why Seeking More Money Hurts Happiness."

[75] Jean Twenge, *Generation Me.*

search consistently refutes the correlation between such pursuits and happiness. Countless social studies link values—not possession, positions or achievements—to well-being. They show that resolutely focusing energy on intrinsic values over extrinsic ones can reduce stress and boost happiness.

These findings are hardly surprising. They have echoed across innumerable faiths and philosophies through the centuries, but many of us choose to buy into the idea that happiness is just another commodity.

Not long ago, on the occasion of the annual Black Friday sales, economist Robert Reich took to his public Facebook page to observe: "In the warped world of business economics, today's Black Friday sales are supposed to indicate the strength of our economy. But the true measure of our well-being isn't how many flat-screen TVs, tablets, smartphones and other stuff we buy today, but how many of us have access to good schools, health care, adequate housing, safe streets, a healthy environment, and jobs paying sufficient wages and offering enough financial security that we can sleep well and give our kids the upbringing they need."

My friend, the author Homa Sabet Tavangar, always observes that very few things in life are inherently evil and that the devil is in how things are sometimes used. And that seems right and true. Consumption is not inherently evil. But unsustainable consumption as a metric of status, worth, value, self-esteem and mental well-being comes close.

Internal Motivations as a Pathway to Meaning

"It is a characteristic of the American culture," wrote Viktor Frankl, "that, again and again, one is commanded and ordered to 'be happy.' But happiness cannot be pursued; it must ensue.

One must have a reason to 'be happy.'" This reason to be happy—this essential "why"—is why we must be resolute in our quest to move beyond extrinsic motivations. Because it is through a life filled with the pursuit of intrinsic motivations that we find the entry points to the pathway to a meaningful and joyful life.

In her *Atlantic* article, "There's More to Life Than Being Happy," Emily Esfahani Smith, a gifted writer who examines various aspects of positive psychology, concluded that while there is a great deal of overlap between happiness and meaning, ultimately a meaningful life is healthier than a happy one. People who lead meaningful lives have stronger immune systems, they have a greater sense of well-being, and they're more resilient. Rather than being an extrinsically motivated "taker," focusing on achieving a meaningful life leads us to being a "giver." "Happiness without meaning characterizes a relatively shallow, self-absorbed or even selfish life, in which things go well, needs and desire are easily satisfied, and difficult or taxing entanglements are avoided," wrote researchers.[76]

As a society, we're seeing the beginnings of a conversation about not defining our well-being solely by economic growth. Increasing numbers believe that gross domestic product as a wealth indicator should be expanded to include well-being and happiness. And similarly, each year the United Nations International Day of Happiness is celebrated with a campaign coordinated by a nonprofit movement of people and organizations from over 140 countries who aim to measure progress by an increase in human happiness and well-being, rather than a growing economy.[77]

---

[76] Quoted in Emily Esfahani Smith, "There's More to Life Than Being Happy," *The Atlantic*, January 9, 2013. Roy F. Baumeister, Kathleen D. Vohs, Jennifer L. Aaker and Emily N. Garbinsky, "Some Key Differences Between a Happy Life and a Meaningful Life," *Journal of Positive Psychology*, August 20, 2013.

[77] www.dayofhappiness.net. See also Moeller, "Why Seeking More Money Hurts Happiness."

Closer to home, individuals and families should invest more time in thinking about their goals, how well they are meeting them and whether they are happy with their choices. Ultimately, true happiness derives from living a daily life that is in accordance with a core set of intrinsic values. It is not based on external praise or validation, but is self-referenced and flows from a core of meaning and service.

The brief exercises below can help you begin to understand where you might fall on the intrinsic-external value scale, and help you to define your life goals and critical measures of well-being.

Practice

- Spend some time alone thinking about the various aspects of the happiness equation.

   Make a clear declaration of the different parts of the formula:

   1. What are your dearest and most important values?
   2. What actually motivates you in your day-to-day life? Is it money? Security? Independence? Your family? Service and volunteerism? Once you are finished, separate the list into two categories, corresponding to whether each one reflects extrinsic or intrinsic motivations, or both.
   3. How do your everyday actions and motivations differ from your internal values?
   4. Consider all the ways the disconnect between your values and your actions is creating destructive stress in your life.

   Reflect on your findings. Is the way you are spending your time serving you and your mission statement? What can you modify or eliminate? Which things would you like to do more of in your life?

- **Find your gratitude.**
  Many studies have shown that experiencing gratitude can make us feel happier and free us from the cycle of constant desire, even if only temporarily. To make gratitude a regular part of your life, consider keeping a bedside gratitude journal. Every so often, jot down at least three things for which you are grateful. Nothing is too small or inconsequential.

- **Share your time.**
  For one week, consciously give the gift of your time—and undivided attention—to three different people for at least fifteen minutes at a time. This gift can take the form of reading, walking or chatting (with a child or adult), or services offered around the house, or time spent helping or sharing a meal with an elderly or infirm neighbor. Remain aware of what you're doing and how you feel afterward.

Rule 6

Be Giving

As far back as Jim McDermott could remember, his mother and father had sat together at the dining room table on the last Friday of every month to pay the bills. And once they had paid the bills, his parents would calculate a percentage of how much they had made that month and would give that away to charity. Jim remembers hearing them discuss at length which charities they were going to support and why.

When Jim and his older sister were teenagers, they were allowed to choose where a small amount of the giving would go. Jim loved sports and was obsessed with physics, but when it came to giving, his interests centered on nature, the environment and conservation.

There were many family discussions about why it was important to give away money and what they thought was being achieved by the gifts they made. His parents spoke about "never letting the right hand know what the left hand is doing"—that is, never advertising the giving. It would be done quietly, they emphasized, without seeking recognition. "In a capitalist society, you invest in the things you believe in, the things you believe have social value," observed Jim's father more than once.

It all became routine for Jim. His father was a physician back then and was also involved in politics part-time. The amount they gave would sometimes go up or down, depending on their needs and income at that moment, but giving became a way of life—something you just did. For them, it was the way to live a balanced, happy life.

The habit stuck. It stayed with Jim through the lean years and the flush years, through college, through business school and, eventually, through the founding of a company he would take public.[78]

"I really believe that giving money in some form or fashion frees you from it," he says. "We are constantly managing money or we're somehow constrained by it. When you have financial pressures, the tendency is to want to hold onto the money at any cost. But the reality is that when you free yourself from that by regularly giving, in some profound ways you are no longer governed by money." Jim is also a realist. He's not naive to the privileged life he now leads. But, he says, even when he didn't have a lot to give, he still gave that same percentage. It was the one constant.

Jim's mother was always a voracious reader with an expansive intellect, and when Jim was in his teens she happened upon a book about something called the "law of tenfold return." Loosely, the idea is that when you give without expectation, it comes back to you tenfold in some form, monetary or otherwise. Jim remembers rolling his eyes at the time and tuning out as his mother described the concept excitedly. Many decades later, he would observe odd coincidences that would remind him of the conversations about the law of tenfold return.

Over the years, Jim has heard about many intangible concepts like chi or karma. "The more I learn about these kinds of ideas," he says, "the more I think that perhaps these people are

---

[78] Jim is one of the founders of Stamps.com.

describing a phenomenon that might have a basis in physics." It may not be immediately intuitive just how, but giving is almost like some law of the universe. Regardless, the energy you send out into the world through service and giving has a profound impact, and that impact is infinitely more potent for you, the giver, than it is for the people you give to.

The principle of giving a percentage of one's income has a foundation in many spiritual doctrines—a tzedakah in Judaism or tithing in Christianity, for example—but the benefits of giving have also been validated by science. The work of Elizabeth Dunn, who has come to be known as the "happy money researcher," is particularly illuminating. Studying money started out for Dunn as what some scientists call "me-search." She had just experienced a major life change in her transition from a poverty-stricken graduate student making under $20,000 a year to having a substantial income. She had been a student of happiness for some time, and she was curious how she might use her newfound wealth to bring greater joy into her life. And as a psychologist, she had the tools at her disposal to look into the question.

She was surprised to see how little research had been conducted on the topic. There was voluminous research on the relationship between income and well-being, but not on how spending smartly and generously could bring greater joy to those who gave. She went on to pioneer the field through a number of fascinating studies on the link between spending and well-being.[79] Dunn's work sheds light on how we can become happier by being generous—and thus reduce destructive stress and anxiety.

Among Dunn's recommendations:[80]

---

[79] While Dunn's studies don't measure stress, they do measure well-being.

[80] Elizabeth Dunn and Michael Norton, *Happy Money: The Science of Smarter Spending*.

➤   If you truly love it, indulge rarely.

➤   Don't spend on yourself; spend on others.

➤   Pay first, consume later.

➤   Buy time.

➤   No to gifts, yes to experiences.

What we choose to spend our money on is closely related to our quest for happiness. We live in a time of dizzying extremes of wealth and poverty. When we can, many of us spend money in an unabashed, carefree way as if doing so would make us happy. Our economic system—supported by media, marketing, advertising and others—encourages and perpetuates this notion.

There is an interesting disconnect here, since most people objectively know that money will not make them happy. But money is something we can all count and as a rule, anything that humans can count, they become obsessed with. The things we can do with money are very physically apparent. "People with more money often even *look* different. So it becomes easy to quantify and compare," says Dunn.

Indulge Rarely

"Go ahead and indulge," drawls the voice in the commercial. "You're worth it!" Indulgence and luxury have become synonymous with the fine art of living in our culture, but Dunn's research finds you should do the opposite. Underindulgence—consuming less, not more—brings far greater satisfaction from money.

Cutting down on consumption can surely be good for our well-being. The core idea in happiness research is that we become accustomed to anything we have repeatedly. A good rule of thumb is to cut down on anything if you no longer look forward to it or even notice it. Abundance is the enemy of appreciation and "having access to the best things in life may actually undermine one's ability to reap enjoyment from life's small pleasures."[81]

In one study, one group of chocolate lovers was given a piece to eat and then agreed not to eat any more for an entire week, while a second group agreed to eat as much chocolate as they could (without getting sick) over the course of week. To assist them with their goal, the second group was provided with a two-pound bag of chocolate. Once the second group returned from their week of indulgence, they reported enjoying chocolate far less than they had the week before. Who enjoyed the confection as much in the second week as they did in the first? Those who had given it up briefly.[82] Dunn points out that even temporarily abstaining can renew the pleasure we derive from many things.

Researchers at Arizona State University conducted a similar experiment. They demonstrated that people who were forced to wait to enjoy their soda—to delay their gratification—enjoyed their drinks significantly more than those who were able to have it right away.

When my son was in second grade, I attended his class holiday party. The seven-year-olds sat in a circle with a pile of Secret Santa presents in the center. As they went around the room calling out names and opening presents one by one, everyone oohed and aahed in support of their friend. The gift budget was ten dol-

---

[81] J. Quoidbach, E. Dunn, et al., "Money Giveth, Money Taketh Away: The Dual Effect of Wealth on Happiness," *Psychological Sciences*, May 2010.

[82] Dunn and Norton, "Don't Indulge. Be Happy."

lars and people had gotten creative. The presents were lovely and thoughtful, funny and fun. About halfway through, a little girl's name was called. Her Secret Santa gift was in a large bag. Everyone oohed and aahed appropriately. She unwrapped box after box from the big bag—four boxes in all—each of them containing what was probably a twenty-five-dollar gift.

The happy energy in the room transformed for everyone.

The little girl who had hit the jackpot: Glee.

The children who *just* got a ten-dollar gift: No longer as gleeful.

The mother of the girl who hit the jackpot: Anxious, making covert hand gestures to her daughter to suppress the child's delight.

The parents of the other kids: Vaguely upset.

There were two questions on every parent's mind: Who was the dolt who had overshot the gift budget? And should I have spent more money too?

The magic of the moment evaporated. Later, a small group of parents was discussing the party.

"What happened back there is what's known as an escalation," I said.

"Yes," agreed another parent. "Someone needs to put up a sign that says: 'Don't be an escalator!'"

Observed a third: "Clearly, more is not always better."

And sometimes, we all agreed, more is just wrong. The issue is that "wrong" has become the norm.

Overindulgence is particularly damaging as it relates to our children. As family dynamics have shifted to more child-centric patterns, very few things are deemed to be too good, too much or too expensive for our kids. And yet our inclination to spoil our offspring can dampen their ability to savor everyday joys. How many times have we heard parents grouse that their children are ungrateful? Is it possible that the parents have an unwitting hand in their children's lack of gratitude? These parents are effectively anesthetizing their children from appreciating what they're given by constantly plying them with everything they ask for. It's a reasonable hypothesis, since providing external rewards for things like jobs well done can inhibit the emotional benefits children get from them. Decades of research show that tangible incentives tend to have a negative effect on intrinsic motivation. According to a review of more than one hundred studies on the effects of rewards, "[e]ven when tangible rewards are offered as indicators of good performance, they typically decrease intrinsic motivation for interesting activities."[83]

Abundance and overindulgence numb us to the greater and more profound joys of life. Many of us have the means to give our children everything, and we think we are doing our kids a favor by making them—and ourselves—feel good. But what we're really doing is robbing them of some of the deepest and most beautiful aspects of humanity. Limiting access to privileges that kids' peers may have in great abundance—sweets, sodas, junk foods, tech gadgets, gaming, phones, TV shows, to name a few—can represent a kind of hardship. But it may also represent a much-needed balance, the meaning of which has been completely warped in our culture. Filling those voids with experiences and opportunities for service can lead to growth, greater happiness and less toxic stress for children.

The very idea of underindulging represents a radical departure from our cultural norms, as does Dunn's next suggestion for how to spend your money: don't spend it on yourself at all!

---

[83] E. L. Deci, R. Koestner and R. Ryan, "A Meta-Analytic Review of Experiments Examining the Effects of Extrinsic Rewards on Intrinsic Motivations," *Psychological Bulletin*, November 1999.

Spend on Others

Consider this scenario: Three people each hit the jackpot and win a million dollars. The first splurges, the second saves and the third gives it all away.

Who's happier?

The second and third winners, says Dunn.[84] Even just thinking about money makes us more focused on ourselves and our own needs, but if we use that money to benefit others, we are able to boost happiness. Interestingly, this is not true just for rich societies. In one study, Dunn and her colleagues observed that the "benefits of prosocial spending are evident in givers old and young in countries around the world." And the reported benefits extend not just to "subjective well-being, but also objective health."[85]

Many find it surprising that this principle also holds true when it comes to children, who are rarely delighted by the prospect of sharing. A study by psychologists at the University of British Columbia found that even young children are happier to give than to receive. In the study, toddlers who were asked to give away their own treats, as well as extra treats, showed greater happiness about sharing their Goldfish crackers, suggesting that the act of personal sacrifice was emotionally rewarding even for the youngest among us. We assume children are inherently selfish and that we need to teach them how to share. As it turns out,

---

[84] Dunn and Norton, "Don't Indulge. Be Happy." and John Tierney, "How to Win the Lottery (Happily)," *New York Times*, May 26, 2014.

[85] E. W. Dunn, L. B. Aknin and M. I. Norton, "Prosocial Spending and Happiness: Using Money to Benefit Others Pays Off," *Current Directions in Psychological Science*, February 2014.

children also are naturally altruistic.[86] More broadly, the study demonstrates the benefits that prosocial spending and behavior can provide, whether that includes volunteering, giving money to causes or otherwise spreading the wealth. All of these correlate to increased happiness.[87]

What's more, prosocial spending can be a virtuous cycle. When people recall a time they spent generously, it makes them happy. That sets up and triggers a positive feedback loop between generous spending and happiness. And while spending money on others leads to higher levels of happiness than spending money on yourself, the amount isn't important. A 2008 study involving students found that spending as little as five dollars on others had emotional benefits.

*   *   *

My husband Jaime grew up in El Paso, Texas, on the border between the United States and Mexico. Years ago, when he was a child, he was riding with his father in their pickup truck. They were driving along when they saw a truck pulled over on the side of the road. The truck's tires were stuck in the mud on the side of the Rio Grande. The driver of the truck and his passenger looked like laborers back from a day's hard work. They were dirty and dusty, standing next to their truck.

My father-in-law pulled over. He retrieved some rope from the back. He connected his truck to the laborers' and helped pull their vehicle out. The laborers had been stuck for a very long time and were so overcome with gratitude that they began looking around for something to give to my father-in-law, but they had nothing to give.

---

[86] J. Kiley Hamlin interview; see also Lara B. Aknin, J. Kiley Hamlin and Elizabeth W. Dunn, "Giving Leads to Happiness in Young Children," *PLoS ONE,* 2012.

[87] See ibid. Lara B. Aknin interview.

One of them looked down on the ground and saw some rocks. He picked up these rocks with both hands and extended them out to my father-in-law. "Please take these rocks," he said. "These are *good* rocks." My father-in-law took the rocks. In a way those rocks, offered with the warmest intentions, became part of his most prized possessions.

Pay Now, Consume Later

"It is literally painful to pay for things!" says Dunn. Studies show that paying a lot for something is akin to physical pain, in terms of the neural response generated. This can be a good thing, because it can help rein in spending. But everything about modern society, including the proliferation of credit cards and apps, propels us toward consuming immediately and paying later. Research suggests that we should be doing the exact opposite: paying up front and then delaying consumption. Say you plan to go on vacation in a few months. Paying for it up front will get the pain of paying out of the way and create a "free" feeling that will make the vacation much more enjoyable.

Also, the biggest happiness boosts come *before* a vacation happens. To the human psyche, the future tends to be more compelling than the past, and looking forward to an upcoming vacation provides a lot more joy than the vacation itself. This is poetically put by Dunn and Norton as "the pleasure of anticipation without the buzzkill of reality."[88]

---

[88] Dunn and Norton, *Happy Money*.

Buy Time

Before you reach for your wallet, stop and ask yourself: How will this purchase affect the way I spend my time? Often the answer will be that it will have no effect. But an interesting idea that has emerged recently is that it may be worthwhile to pay your way out of those tasks you dread most. People tend to overestimate how much it will cost to outsource their most dreaded tasks. A good strategy may be that, if it's financially feasible, you should consider outsourcing (buying your way out of) those tasks you despise and that take up too much of your time or that fill you with anxiety.

Buy Experiences, Not Gifts

People get more lasting happiness from buying experiences like trips, concerts or special meals than they do from buying material things. "That principle can range from couches to cars to houses," says Dunn.

Our relationship with money can contribute to a wholly unsustainable culture ruled by destructive, chronic stress. It is possible to spend money in a way to help us become happier and less burdened. Dunn's strategies paint a compelling picture that may help us rethink some of our over-the-top spending habits. Her research also confirms some age-old wisdom about wealth and money: If our goal really is to make ourselves—and our children—happy, we ought to be doing something very different with our money.

Practice

- **Challenge yourself to spend mindfully.**

  When we consider mindfulness, most of us think of yoga,
  meditation and even mindful eating—not the way we spend
  money. But our spending habits are often mindless and automatic,
  as we dig ourselves further and further into debilitating debt.[89]
  Embarking upon a mindfulness practice when it comes to
  spending can dramatically influence destructive stress patterns in
  our lives.

  It also provides us with a greater sense of control. It introduces
  an individually driven, spiritual aspect of the solution to our larger
  economic problems and gives each of us the opportunity to reflect
  on, and gain important insights about, our relationship with
  money.

  Dr. Jan Chozen Bays, author of *How to Train a Wild Elephant
  and Other Adventures in Mindfulness*, believes that most of us
  would be well served by practicing greater mindfulness in all
  areas of our lives, including spending. Her suggestions for
  exercising conscious, mindful spending include:

  - **Surf the urge.**

    Every time the impulse arises to buy something, ask
    yourself: Do I really, truly need this? Do I need it now?
    This is "surfing the urge." When the urge arises to
    acquire something, surf it, and stay with it for a while.
    How many times have you thought, "I need one of

---

[89] Elizabeth Dunn's research shows that debt is one of the most potent joy
killers.

these things," but for some reason you can't get to the store. Then, later, you can't even recall what it was you needed. The urge that seemed so compelling at the time disappeared entirely. Build in a delay while you question whether you truly need to make the purchase. What are the alternatives to buying? What if you saved the money instead?

- **Question the desire.**
  We have this notion that our desires need to be satisfied right away, this urgent need for instant gratification. But, Bays asks, what is the need you are trying to fulfill? Are you really hungry? Are you anxious? Do you need a distraction? You must determine whether what you want to buy will truly make you happy, or if it will just keep the endless wheel of desire going.

- **Avoid habitual momentum.**
  We can get caught in our habits and keep going along a well-worn track, but momentum often comes from habit and impulse, not from being present. Become more conscious and deliberate about spending habits.[90]

- **Stay with discomfort.**
  Life is not always comfortable, and many of us have a problem being present with that reality. It's so easy to be disconnected. We get caught in our thoughts and worries, and in what we think will fill up the space and take away pain. But you will encounter suffering in life.

---

[90] Lee Lesser, teacher of sensory awareness.

We try to deny that, to buy our way out of it—but of course we can't. None of us can, not even the wealthy. Mindfulness teaches us that there is no place to go but here, in the present moment. When we are able to focus on the present, the discomfort changes and we can offer attention to things in a way that is meaningful and comforting.

- **Rest in your breath.**
  When you're in the uncomfortable moment of resisting your habits and urges, reflect, pause and focus on your breathing. Becoming mindful of your breath can be profoundly comforting. Use the sensation of your breath as an anchor for consciousness in the present moment. You may eventually widen this awareness to include other senses—sight, sound, smell, touch and taste.

- **Offer real intimacy.**
  Resist the idea that you can make yourself and your loved ones happy by buying them stuff. "What we really want, what our children really want, is true intimacy, a sense of connectedness," says Bays. Research shows that such intimacy reduces stress and protects us during traumatic times. A sense of security reduces stress hormone levels in the body.

- **Value your life's energy.**
  Ultimately, money is a symbol of energy. It's a way to buy and trade energy. Before you make any purchase, ask yourself whether it's worth your effort and your

(or someone else's) life's energy. Would you prefer to use it to buy yet another pair of shoes, or would you rather spend it in another way? Save it perhaps, or use it to take a trip that may change you or expand who you are in some substantial way? Perhaps you decide you prefer the shoes, and that's fine. Just be sure you're making that decision consciously.

- **Opt for true satisfaction.**
  In the end, we all want to be happy. But it's not the happiness we see in advertisements, on a roller coaster laughing hysterically and holding up a can of soda! We want the simple, authentic kind of happiness, the kind that does not come from material possessions. There are things we need to sustain ourselves. For everything else, pause and consciously consider: Will this buy me happiness? Or will it contribute to more stress, anxiety and dysfunction?

Rule 7

Be Kind

Let us always meet each other with a smile, for the smile is the beginning of love.

—MOTHER TERESA

Most Sundays Juliet Jones[91] woke up feeling fine. But as the day wore on, she grew more agitated. By early afternoon she felt almost sick with stress, walking around snapping at everyone. It was an odd thing, mostly because Juliet is about as optimistic and sunny as people come. It was her husband who finally figured out what was happening. Juliet was dreading going back to work on Monday morning. And the anticipation was ruining not just her day, but the entire family's.

Juliet worked at a pharmaceutical company founded and run by a handful of idealists. She loved her job, until the company was bought out. The culture of the organization shifted overnight. The scientists who had founded the company were pushed out. In came the new leadership team, made up of corporate marketing types who had a new agenda and were out to set an entirely different tone.

---

[91] Name has been changed.

"It's as if the entire company was caught in the grips of stress. Constant, endless stress," Juliet recalled. The new executives were like stress funnels, she observed, spreading anxiety through every aspect of work. Toward the end, the atmosphere was just unbearable. What's worse, Juliet's misery began to bleed into her everyday home life.

The company went downhill fast. It began to hemorrhage its best employees. Juliet's colleagues, most of the old guard—the most talented and devoted scientists in the group—despaired for a long time. And then they left in droves. Eventually, she left too.

The Blessing and the Curse

Our radical interconnectedness has been lauded as one of the great achievements of our age. It is an innovation that has brought with it many blessings. It has also enabled the chronic and pervasive cultural narrative of stress to gain a constant foothold in our lives through an age-old human propensity to pass feelings to one another: This is known as "emotional contagion." According to a recent study, what was once six degrees of separation between any two people in the world has shrunk to 4.74—three, if you limit the pair to a particular country. Interconnectedness is also not without its dark sides. Being constantly connected to friends and family through a multitude of devices and platforms ensures that stress is shared and multiplied. Your stress is not just your own; it's effectively yours, your friends', your family's, and can affect just about everyone else who comes into contact with you. We volley emotions back and forth all the time, as part of every interaction—however brief or extended—that we have with each another. We can "catch" other people's stress, all with amazing speed.

Catching Emotions

In many important ways, we humans are open books. It was psychologist Paul Ekman who first identified a series of universal emotions—surprise, anger, fear, happiness, disgust and sadness (and later, contempt)—that form the basis of nonverbal communication among all humans, regardless of nationality or culture. Ekman and his colleagues also discovered that even when people are attempting to conceal their emotions, their involuntary "microexpressions" give away their true feelings.

Scientists had long known that humans transfer emotions to one another. But it was psychologist Elaine Hatfield who pioneered the field by bringing together many of the pieces of the puzzle of emotional contagion.

Hatfield's first inkling came through her work as a therapist. She noticed that her moods changed following her appointments, often reflecting those of her clients. A similar dynamic was at play with colleagues. She came to realize that she was, somehow, "catching" the emotions of those she interacted with.[92]

Hatfield and her colleagues went on to discover that, "from infancy, all of us imitate facial expressions, postures and voices of the people around us. Those expressions trigger certain emotions—the same ones experienced by the person we mimic." Hatfield's early research showed that newborns are capable of vocal and movement mimicry. "Mimicry is a basic biological mechanism that may confer an evolutionary advantage. . . . It helps you understand what another person is feeling and thinking—even when

---

[92] Dorothy Foltz-Gray, "How Contagious Are Your Emotions?," *O, The Oprah Magazine,* December 2004.

he or she is trying to hide it."[93] In one classic study, two- to four-day-olds responded to the emotional stress of other newborns by crying as well. They did not respond similarly when they heard a synthetic cry. How quickly can contagious stress spread? The research is varied, but it can happen with amazing speed. We can respond to people's faces faster than we can have a thought. Hatfield suggests that it's so primitive that it's probably going through the brain stem.

Many believe that empathy lies at the root of emotional contagion. Researchers have found that a person's stress hormone levels can rise simply by watching someone else experience stress.[94] This is particularly true for married couples.[95] In fact, in-person interaction may not even be necessary—watching stressful moments on TV might be enough to raise cortisol levels. Following 9/11, for example, some people who didn't experience the actual events firsthand were affected by post-traumatic stress. The severity appeared to correlate to how much television they watched.

A New Wrinkle: Contagion Through Social Networks

A recent study adds an alarming nuance to the picture: Emotions can spread rapidly among users of online social networks.

Previous experiments hinted at the possibility that online interactions led to emotional contagion, but a collaboration between social scientists at Cornell University, UC San Francisco and Face-

---

[93] Peter Tottendale, PhD, quoted in Foltz-Gray, "How Contagious Are Your Emotions?"

[94] Amanda Chan, "Yes, Your Stress Really Is Rubbing Off on Everyone Around You," Huffington Post, May 5, 2014.

[95] "Emotional contagion sweeps Facebook, finds new study," Science Daily, June 13, 2014.

book shows online moods can be just as contagious as real-life ones.[96] Researchers randomly selected almost seven hundred thousand Facebook users and reduced the number of either positive or negative stories in their news feed. The impact of emotional contagion worked in both positive and negative ways: Those exposed to negative content for a week went on to use more negative words in their status updates, and those exposed to positive content used significantly more positive words. Moreover, users' online moods also predicted their friends' moods, even up to several days later.

The effect also extended offline: Users exposed to fewer emotional posts were less expressive in real life in the days that followed.

Stress Influencers

When we talk about stress, we are usually referring to how *we* feel. But a critical aspect of stress is how *we* are stressing *others*. Because of the principle of emotional contagion, navigating stress on a day-to-day basis requires a sense of responsibility, an honor system of sorts, toward the collective energy. Reducing the pervasive destructive stress many suffer from requires both consciousness of negativity and incivility, and the adoption of personal responsibility for the energy we bring to our daily circumstances.

Jill Bolte Taylor, our brain scientist who suffered a stroke in her left brain, recalled that as she lay recovering in her hospital bed, she was able to distinguish the doctors and nurses who walked into her room by their energy, either positive or negative. She now believes that we are each personally responsible for the

---

[96] A. Kramer, J. Guillory and J. Hancock, "Experimental Evidence of Massive Scale Emotional Contagion Through Social Networks," *Proceedings of the National Academy of the Sciences*, June 17, 2014.

energy we bring into a space. "You are responsible for the energy you create for yourself," she has observed, "and you're responsible for the energy you bring to others."

Are some people particularly influential in the stress epidemic? Do key influencers contribute to a culture of anxiety by helping to set a negative emotional tone that infects our collective well-being?

Take emotional contagion and greater connectivity, and add people in key positions of influence—so-called connectors, such as our bosses, politicians, media, teachers. A notable few wield their power to inspire, enlighten and advance, but far too many perpetuate a climate of negativity.

Some of these stress influencers are merely passive, thoughtless and irresponsible, while others are actively manipulative and self-serving. Either way, by virtue of their power positions, these people can wreak havoc by spreading anxiety. It is a pattern of behavior perhaps most damaging during times of hardship, when it's most prevalent.

Balance in the Face of Contagious Stress

It may seem impossible to seek serenity in a world affected by the very real anxieties about economic troubles, environmental disasters, political discord, wars and terrorism, especially when these are whipped into an engineered frenzy by the sky-is-falling politicians and talk show hosts who permeate the media.

According to psychologist James Gross, an expert on emotional regulation, there are two key ways to push through the noise of stress, both real and manufactured.

First, the effects of stress are compounded by the fact that we are rarely turned off and are always connected. Stress in its various forms has access to us at all times. In the old days people got upset and were able to go for a walk to get away. Now we are never far from all sorts of bad news. The solution: turn it off! Go on technology fasts. Embargo most news during the most vitriolic and heated period of a crisis.

The other key idea is to acknowledge that we have considerable control over the emotions and stress that we feel, even when it doesn't feel that way. We have the power to remain conscious in the moment and to choose our perceptions. We can choose narratives that help us reframe stressors, thereby strengthening our ability to withstand (or avoid) the stress coming our way and to counter it with positive emotions. Or recognize that awkward or unfamiliar feelings may not be us at all—it may be someone else having a tough time.

Ultimately, we are masters of our inner world, famed psychologist Daniel Goleman and author of *Emotional Intelligence* once told me. We can intentionally practice methods for relaxation that will counter the stress of negativity. The more we practice, the better it works as an inoculation against toxic environments. It's important to find a relaxation method that works for you and practice it daily—the same way you would an exercise routine.

Fortunately, there's also a flipside of contagious stress: countercontagion. That is, contagious joy, happiness, bliss. Emotional contagion applies to positive emotions as well. When we're with an upbeat person, we're likely to catch their mood too, and happily so. Because it serves as a perfect transition to that thing most of us would like to see go viral: love, kindness and civility.

The Decline of Civility

> This is my simple religion. There is no need for temples; no
> need for complicated philosophy. Our own brain, our own
> heart is our temple; the philosophy is kindness.
>
> —DALAI LAMA

As we consider civility and kindness, and their relationship to the
pervasive sense of stress many of us are feeling in our lives, perhaps we should turn our attention to divisive incidents like the
shooting death of young Michael Brown in Ferguson, Missouri,
on August 9, 2014. With a community deeply at odds and pro-
tests nationwide, many of us stood witness to the heartbreak,
anger and outrage unfolding in our lives, on our streets and on
our screens.

We are a young and diverse nation, populated by many races,
faiths, nationalities and orientations, and so we are often forced
to face and accept the reality that our perceptions and experiences vary. We all see life and circumstances differently—sometimes in subtle ways and sometimes in dramatically different
ways. The trouble, though, is when unkindness, incivility and a
horrifying absence of empathy become placeholders for legitimate discourse and disagreement.

In reality it matters very little where each of us falls on the social and political issues of our day. If we are not approaching the
situation first and foremost with love and kindness, we are lost. If
we can't accept that there are many, many different ways to experience and interpret the exact same event, we are lost. If we can't
mourn tragedies like a young life cut short under tragic circumstances, we are lost. If we can't even begin to muster empathy for
our friends and neighbors, our brethren who are heartbroken, out-
raged, distressed and devastated, we are lost.

And when we look at our lives, and times and lament *all the stress,* and look at our society, town, state, country and world, and mourn its decline, we must know that this is in large part what our own hands have wrought. And that we have the power to change that by entering every moment of our lives love first.

♦ ♦ ♦

A majority of us believe that civility is declining in our culture. A 2010 National Civility Survey found that two out of three Americans believe civility is a major issue, and three in four believe the negative tenor in our country has grown worse over the past few years. All indications are that our divisions have grown even deeper (and the tone more vitriolic) since the survey was conducted. While unkind, incivil people have been around forever, the perception that their numbers are growing serves as a chronic, low-grade stressor in daily life, no matter where we encounter them.

Dr. Piero Forni is the director of the Civility Initiative at Johns Hopkins and author of *The Civility Solution: What to Do When People Are Rude.* He studies the link between everyday stress and civility, with the viewpoint that being kind, loving and civil to others serves both society and ourselves.

Kinder people tend to live longer and lead healthier lives, volunteers have fewer aches and pains, and compassionate people are more likely to be healthier and successful. Echoing the science supporting love, research shows that when we engage in acts of civility and kindness—like offering a seat on the train to a disabled person or helping an elderly person cross the street—both the person on the giving end and the one on the receiving end benefit from a calm, euphoric feeling known as "helper's high." During helper's high, cascades of hormones and neurotransmitters activate, followed by an improved sense of well-being.

Widespread incivility, on the other hand, can wreak havoc. Mean people, writes Stanford professor Robert Sutton, have "devastating effects, partly because nasty interactions have a far bigger impact on our moods than positive interactions—five times the punch." As a result of emotional contagion, the effects of negative interactions adversely affect coworkers, family members and friends who witness, or even just hear about, the incidents.

Sutton has written widely about the economic and social benefits of rooting out jerks from the workplace in his bestselling book *The No Asshole Rule: Building a Civilized Workplace and Surviving One That Isn't*. He distinguishes between occasional rudeness—of which everyone is more or less guilty every so often—and certified jerks.

But why are people unkind? Forni suggests a handful of root causes that may cover the entire spectrum of uncivilized behavior: lack of empathy and restraint, stress, illness, depression, anonymity, insecurity, lack of time, a sense of entitlement.

These factors can work together, says Forni. In traffic, for example, anonymity and stress work together. The first driver cuts off the second driver. Perhaps both are late and therefore anxious. They don't think they know each other, and so they engage in what Forni colorfully calls "finger puppetry." But should one of the drivers suddenly recognize the other as someone he knows—a neighbor, perhaps, or the pastor from church—civility prevails and there will be an immediate effort by the offending party to minimize what has happened.

Anonymity also plays into uncivil behavior online: "You have this wonderful technological marvel that can improve our lives, and yet it has become a dismal collector of the moral toxins of our society," Forni observes.

Ultimately, civility is about love, empathy, power and character. "The difference between how a person treats the powerless versus the powerful is as good a measure of human character as I know," writes Sutton.

Loving-Kindness Meditation

The loving-kindness meditation, or compassion meditation, is a powerful but incredibly simple practice that involves directing a series of phrases that carry well wishes toward oneself and other people—not just those who are easy to love, but also those who may be far less so. The meditation originated as part of a series of four Buddhist virtues—love, compassion, joy and equanimity—and the practices created to cultivate them, called the brahmaviharas, or sublime attitudes.

The tangible and dramatic impact of the loving-kindness meditation has been validated through various research that shows that it increases people's experiences of positive emotions and places people on "trajectories of growth," leaving them better able to ward off depression and "become more satisfied with life." Research also shows that the meditation "changes the way people approach life" for the better.[97] It can be practiced daily and with very little training.

The meditation comes in many forms, both formal and informal. On a recent morning, author Elizabeth Gilbert took to her Facebook page: "Are you searching for the light?" she asked. "Be the light." She then shared her take on the practice: "I began a simple practice, of steadfastly wishing blessings upon every person I encountered. I was living in New York City at the time, where you encounter lots of people a day, so that was a good

---

[97] "Greater Happiness in Five Minutes a Day," Greater Good Science Center, September 10, 2012, http://greatergood.berkeley.edu/raising_happiness/post/better_than_sex_and_appropriate_for_kids.

place to practice . . . I would silently say to [each] human being, 'May you know happiness. May you be free from suffering.'"[98]

The version of the loving-kindness meditation I share below comes courtesy of the extraordinary Trudy Goodman, founder and guiding teacher of InsightLA, a nonprofit organization for meditation training and secular mindfulness education.

The loving-kindness meditation is a way to grow our capacity to love, says Goodman. She also calls the meditation by other names, such as "blessings," "prayers" or even this mouthful: "wishes for ourselves and all beings to be safe, happy, healthy and free." The idea is not that you are transforming the person, but that you are freeing yourself from dwelling in the space of resentment or ill will, or bearing grudges, all of which influence chronic stress and well-being.

Goodman's meditation phrases are more nuanced and cover a range of well wishes that include having an open heart, living with contentment and being free from suffering, worries, anxieties and destructive stress. "They are not affirmations, but aspirations," says Goodman. "Sometimes in affirmations, we are trying to say we are a certain way when we are not, and there is a conflict. Our aspirations are what we wish to be."

Often when we decide to grow our capacity for love, we encounter everything that is not of love in our being. This meditation is also used to bring more tenderness and kindness to the experiences we have that are not loving or kind. The meditation was initially taught as a powerful antidote to fear and anger. The Buddha taught it as a way to walk in the world without fear.

---

[98] I highly recommend reading Ms. Gilbert's post in its entirety. You can find the link in Selected Resources.

To begin the loving-kindness meditation, sit quietly as you would with any meditation.

Take a series of deep breaths to bring yourself into being and fully present. As you repeat the phrases below, Goodman recommends that you put your energy, through a pointed focus, into saying the mantras.

First you offer the meditation phrases to yourself.

And then to a mentor or benefactor who has helped you in this life.

Then to a friend.

Next you offer the phrases to someone who is very neutral to you, about whom you don't feel much, but you learn to offer them loving kindness.

And finally you direct loving kindness to difficult people, who may be bringing a degree of difficulty or tension into your life.

Select and Use the Four Loving-Kindness Meditation Phrases That Resonate Most with You

- May I/you/all beings be safe and protected from inner and outer harm.

- May I/you/all beings be truly happy and deeply peaceful.

- May I/you/all beings live with the ease of an open heart.

- May my/your/all heart(s) be steady through the ups and downs of life.

- May I/you/all beings have the inner resources needed to meet each moment as a friend.

- May I/you/all beings have the support needed to be present for others.

- May I/you/all beings appreciate life completely, just as it is.

- May I/you/all beings love myself/yourself/themselves completely, just the way I am/you are/they are.

- May I/you/all beings be healthy and strong.

- May I/you/all beings be well, and if that's not possible, may I/you/all beings accept my/your/our limitations with grace.

Practice

Since stress funnels are unavoidable, Sutton offers a few tips on how to deal with them—and perhaps rebound more quickly from run-ins:

- **Stand up or develop indifference.**
  If you find yourself the victim of bad behavior, do a power analysis: You can either address the problem directly or you can

exercise the fine art of emotional detachment. If it's a traffic encounter, can you take a picture of the person's license plate and report him to the police? Is there a number on the side of the vehicle that you can call? If yes, fine. If not, then try to forget the incident as quickly as possible. There are times when things are beyond your control and the best thing for your mental health is to not give a damn.

- **Reframe and change how you see things.**
  Attempt to reframe a run-in with a jerk in a way that is less upsetting. This is a form of mini cognitive therapy. If you can't escape a stressor, you can reduce the damage by changing your mindset about it. Develop a coping mechanism, if you must, because sometimes we are able to find delusions that serve us. Here's an example: Imagine a holiday meal in which a relative does something rude. You can let it ruin the night and complain afterward. Or you can divert your attention from the one percent that was bad and not allow it to ruin the 99 percent that was good. Reframing can be surprisingly effective. A caution, however: Reframing will not make a long-term problem go away.

- **Limit your exposure.**
  Avoid if you need to. For example, if you shop at the same place frequently, go out of your way to avoid the mean clerks. By limiting how often and intensely you face jerks, you create a buffer against their demeaning behavior. In a work context, Sutton offers additional strategies, like building pockets of safety, support and sanity; and seeking and fighting battles that you have a good chance of winning.

CHAPTER EIGHT

Your Body

As an example to others, and not that I care for moderation myself, it has always been my rule never to smoke when asleep, and never to refrain when awake.

—MARK TWAIN

Rule 8

Be Healthy

Eat food. Not too much. Mostly plants.

—MICHAEL POLLAN

The day I was diagnosed with late-stage cancer, I changed my diet. That same day. Not an easy thing to do after a lifetime of scanning the dessert menu *before* the dinner menu, and consuming a steady diet of breads and coffees and cakes and candy bars and burgers and—oh, that first, delightfully fresh and fizzy swig of soda!

Lucky me, I remember thinking once, years before I got sick. *I don't have a weight problem and so I can eat whatever I want.*

For decades now, we have been needless subscribers to the "modern American diet," or MAD diet (which is mad indeed). As we become further buried under the havoc of being overweight, we miss the second—perhaps even more catastrophic—impact of the foods we eat: our mental health. Most of us know that the American diet is linked to epidemics of obesity and diabetes, but few of us are aware that it may also contribute significantly to the skyrocketing level of brain disorders, observes Dr. Drew Ramsey, author of *The Happiness Diet.*

All those "happy" meals, it turns out, are anything but.

The foods we eat day in and day out can undermine our emotional and mental well-being. We *know* this—most of us grasp intuitively that food can influence physical and mental health. We are what we eat, and so on . . . So where is the disconnect?

The disconnect is in the gradual erosion of moderation. Every oncologist I spoke to about my intention to cut out processed foods and sugar from my diet told me to eat "moderately." I was unclear what exactly this meant.

I have also noticed that when playground discussions turn to the alarming amount of sugar and processed foods our children consume daily, the mothers of those kids who eat junk food with the greatest abandon are often the ones who give a beatific smile and a shrug as they observe: "Our rule is 'Everything in moderation.'"

What does "moderation" mean in immoderate times?

This is an important question that we all must consciously ask ourselves in our quest to bring greater balance into our lives. What we eat is a key enabler in the cycle of chronic stress that keeps our bodies constantly flooded with the stress hormone cortisol and in a perpetual state of inflammation.

Emotional well-being also requires greater awareness of what we put into our bodies, and the impact food has on us. A balanced diet of mostly unprocessed foods helps us deal with stress optimally and gain the upper hand over inevitable stressors. Consuming better foods helps us escape the highs and lows of binges and crashes that can taint our perception of the challenges that come our way. Living a balanced life begins with eating a balanced diet.

Food has a direct effect on the biology of stress—of particular concern, of course, because of the link between stress and chronic disease. While we have long known about the connection between addiction and stress, and how stress can increase our susceptibility to chronic diseases, scientists have only recently started to understand the biological mechanisms. You will recall that stressors trigger the evolutionary fight-or-flight response, in which the whole body gears up to move quickly to get out of danger. When the body produces cortisol in this process, and releases glucose and insulin to power our muscles so they can deal with the stress, it is taxing the prefrontal cortex of the brain, crucial for maintaining balance. The prefrontal cortex, remember, is also responsible for impulses, emotions, desires and cognition.

It's a feed-forward model in which stress begets more stress. High-fat, high-calorie junk foods (seen by many as comfort foods), and substances like alcohol, nicotine and cocaine can serve as powerful modifiers of the stress system. They change our stress pathways and affect the way we are able to control our response to new stress triggers.

Self-medicate with junk food and you will intensify destructive stress patterns. Do it over the long term, and you will trap yourself in a vicious cycle that will shape your mood and stress levels from inside out.[99]

The Food-Mood-Food Cycle

Our scientific grasp of the connection between food and mood has expanded dramatically since Hippocrates, the father of medicine, declared over two thousand years ago: "Let your food be your medicine, and your medicine be your food." We now understand the means by which some foods modify the brain's chemistry and physiology and how those, in turn, impact stress.

That foods can soothe, reduce anxiety and boost your mood

---

[99] Dr. Rajita Sinha, Yale Stress Center; Dr. Dew Ramsey, professor of psychiatry at Columbia University; and see Tyler G. Graham and Ramsey, *The Happiness Diet*.

is well-known to anyone who has demolished a pint of Chunky Monkey at the end of a day gone awry. And in a perverse way, ice cream and chips do represent a fast track to happiness. Foods that directly impact brain neurotransmitters have the biggest effect on mood. A load of simple carbohydrates, for example, provides an instant lift because carbohydrates trigger the rapid release of serotonin, the mood-elevating "happy hormone." When the brain produces serotonin, we experience a calming effect.

But a simple carb overload also sets off a physiological chain reaction that wreaks havoc on the body. It taxes the adrenal glands, suppresses the immune system for hours after intake and generally leaves a person feeling sluggish and off-kilter. And then there's the sugar crash.

Robin Kanarek of the Friedman School of Nutrition Science and Policy at Tufts University studies the psychology of stress eating. "Food is more than nutrition," she says. "It can have nutritional value, but it also has cultural and social value. Sometimes our beliefs about food may be influencing behavior as much as the nutrition."

When it comes to food and mood, cognitive factors such as expectations, past experiences or current circumstances can trump even physiology. Take, for example, how we relate to what we think of as comfort foods, or how certain wafting aromas can trigger desire, stress or other strong emotions, either positive or negative. And also consider how dieters consumed by feelings of guilt, anxiety and remorse after indulging in so-called forbidden foods can become derailed by their emotional reactions, even when their initial indulgence was objectively innocuous.

In one of Kanarek's studies, students were given either a doughnut or a banana, each with an equal number of calories and sugar grams. The students who received a doughnut reported feeling worse about themselves and their body image after they ate it. In another study, subjects were provided with a milk shake, with one group being told it was high in calories and the other being told it was low. Those who thought they were consuming a high-calorie shake were much more likely to double down and indulge in Ring Dings (frosted cream-filled devil's food cakes) afterward. Their thinking was, "I've already messed up, so I might as well keep eating."

Another side effect of stress eating is that your brain becomes conditioned to want those cookies, bagels, chips and doughnuts. Over time, your brain creates reward pathways. Come two or three p.m., you're craving those empty calories. That's when you become vulnerable, because once those reward pathways have been created, willpower alone is not going to work very well anymore. What then?

You can create new pathways and new happy memories by finding other ways of channeling the energy and coping. When afternoon comes and those cravings strike, consider getting up and taking a short walk, or a series of deep breaths, which will also help lower cortisol levels. Maybe you really are hungry, in which case you need to eat something both satisfying and nutritious. Kanarek recommends having healthy snacks handy if you tend to have an afternoon lull. "If you're stressed out and all you can find is junk food from the vending machine down the hall, you may start a cycle that can lead to even more stress," she says. Having fruits and vegetables readily available lets you indulge in something sweet that tastes good and has nutritional value, without the snowball effect.

Food, Addiction and Chronic Stress

What do drug addicts, serial dieters and children from troubled homes have in common?

Toxic stress plays a destructive role in triggering a vicious cycle that leaves them with uncontrollable impulses and distracted by negative feelings. Overwhelmed, they succumb to their impulses, which then spark subsequent cycles of relapse, bingeing and failure.

In 1994 Dr. Rajita Sinha was running the substance abuse treatment unit at Yale. As the clinical director, she was doing research on cognitive behavioral treatments that taught recovering addicts how to identify problems and overcome cravings. Although the research showed that these strategies worked, they tended to have only modest effects—a number of people benefited, but it was not particularly significant. Sinha ran group counseling in her clinic and saw the same individuals come back over and over again. They would tell her, "I know what I'm supposed to do. I have these skills, but when I'm out there and something happens, I just can't help myself."

The biggest challenge with addiction is relapse, so Sinha set out to understand what drives it. What brought addictive behaviors back? It became clear to her that there was often a threshold moment during which some kind of challenge or trigger prevented the recovering person from accessing his or her cognitive resources. The way emotions were flooding the person somehow led to a greater risk of relapse.

In each case, Sinha observed that stress played a pivotal role in the loss of control. Sinha and her colleagues set out to replicate the behavior in a laboratory setting to study firsthand the effects of stress on control over urges. They began to bring addicted people in recovery into the lab and give them a series of challenges in controlled experiments. They found that when addicted individuals were under stress, they almost automatically wanted to start using drugs again.

The research began to establish a clear pattern of stress-induced craving for drugs, both for those early in recovery and for those who were still actively using. And it wasn't just higher levels of anxiety and negative emotions that were making the recovering addicts use drugs in search of relief; in parallel, the stress was actually escalating the craving for the drug. Subsequent experiments showed that stress led to the loss of self-control across a spectrum of behaviors, including among people addicted to food, gambling, tobacco and alcohol.

Sinha and her colleagues started to look into the brain to see what was happening and found that, during periods of arousal, the "habit" regions in the brain were activated. The researchers spent a lot of time examining this mechanism in an attempt to figure out how to break the cycle of addiction. As it turns out, we have many habits that are important for survival. Habits form evolutionarily hardwired responses that come from a primitive need to respond very quickly, and it's difficult to break that link.

The good news about habits is that while they often work against us, they can also work for us. When you are stressed and overwhelmed, or simply lack willpower, you are more likely to engage in bad habits. But what happens when it involves your good habits? Scientists have found that it's exactly the same thing: We are more likely to revert to them.[100]

Across a series of five experiments, UCLA researchers showed

---

[100] David T. Neal, Wendy Wood and Aimee Drolet, "How Do People Adhere to Goals When Willpower Is Low? The Profits (and Pitfalls) of Strong Habits," *Journal of Personality and Social Psychology*, June 2013.

that when people are stressed-out and tired, they return to their fundamental routines—whether those are good or bad.[101] One study found that students undergoing exams increased their performance of both desirable and undesirable habits. That is, those students who regularly ate healthy foods for breakfast were more likely to do so during exam time. Students used to eating an unhealthy breakfast—pastries, pancakes, French toast—were similarly inclined. The scientists also found that students in the habit of reading an educational section of the newspaper were more likely to continue reading the paper during their exam weeks, as were those students who read entertaining or less informative sections of the paper. This pattern was especially noteworthy because the increase in "habitual reading emerged despite the greater time demands that students experience during exam weeks."

A well-established body of research tells us that willpower is a finite resource. In the face of multiple stressful stimuli, our willpower wears out and it takes time—and sometimes sleep—to recover. Say you're having a conversation with your mother-in-law and you're stifling some things you really want to say. That's one form of willpower. If at the same time you're sitting near a plate of fresh hot chocolate chip cookies and you're trying to prevent yourself from overindulging, that represents another form of willpower. Though they are very different types of self-regulation, both draw from the same well, making it more challenging for you to control either action. Thankfully, it doesn't necessarily follow that you will tell off your mother-in-law and stuff your face with cookies.

When you lack willpower, you avoid anything new and fall back on what you already know—in other words, you revert to your default settings, and most of us have more good default hab-

---

[101] Ibid.

its than bad. People associate habits with unwanted behaviors, but the mechanism behind automatically reverting to undesirable habits is the same as that behind desirable habits. We just tend to focus on our bad habits because they are such a challenge. We don't realize that many of our daily habits are actually beneficial and help us to meet goals.[102]

Tough as it seems, it is possible to shift bad habits.[103] There are two steps here: first, breaking the bad habit; then, establishing a new habit in its place.

Simple techniques that may help include:[104]

➤ **Changing the environment.** Many of our bad habits are context-cued. By changing our environment, we can remove the cues that may be problematic. If a visual trigger is not present, we may not, for example, unconsciously reach for unhealthy foods. Out of sight, out of mind . . .

➤ **Plan ahead.** Since the unconscious mind is extremely cue-driven, we can use the conscious mind to stack the deck in our favor. Keeping healthy snacks in the car or at your desk, for example, may encourage you to grab those when you're hungry.

➤ **Disrupt established patterns.** Changing the sequence of actions in a daily habit can change the habit. One study showed that this

---

[102] Neal interview.

[103] One of my favorite books on this topic is *The Power of Habit* by Charles Duhigg.

[104] David T. Neal, Wendy Wood, Mengju Wu and David Kurlander, "The Pull of the Past: When Do Habits Persist Despite Conflict with Motives?" *Personality and Social Psychology Bulletin*, November 2011.

can be as simple as switching the hand with which you eat from the dominant hand to the nondominant one.[105]

How to Eat

Why do so many of us struggle to maintain a moderate, balanced regimen when it comes to our food? The reasons are many, and they are complex and interwoven. There is the human perception that it is easier (at least in the short term) to walk the path of least resistance, to accept and do what's easiest, which often corresponds to what "everyone else" is doing. But this kind of passivity and undeliberate living is exactly what's propelled us into our ruinous food-mood-food cycle, always feeding the urge right in front of us without considering the bigger impact on well-being.

Other factors include education ("when you know better, you do better"), socioeconomics and the politics of cheap processed foods. Not to mention the whiplash of clashing public information—and misinformation—campaigns, and differing scientific opinions. In a page taken directly from the tobacco companies' playbook, the corporate food interests that profit from our continuing reliance on their products have only orchestrated, fed and perpetuated the problem.[106]

I am often told by people that they have given up trying to eat a healthy diet because they no longer know what to eat. "Every week you hear something different," they say. This is what I call "contradicting research fatigue." One of the most recent illustra-

---

[105] Ibid.

[106] Michael Moss's book *Salt, Sugar, Fat* is a jaw-dropping look at how the food industry has spent nearly a century distorting the American diet in favor of products that have contributed to a calamitous rise in obesity and disease.

tions is butter, a villain for the better half of the past half century due to its saturated-fat content, but redeemed not long ago when it was found that the alternative, trans fats, were even worse. Soon headlines were declaring: "Butter Is Back!"

The breakthrough for award-winning dietitian and nutritionist Manuel Villacorta came in the kitchen. In the first few years after he moved to the United States from Peru in the 1980s, he was stressed and couldn't shake the sense that something was missing from his life. "One day, I was thinking about what I was going to eat for lunch and I realized that I could not face one more sandwich or salad," he said. "What was missing were my mother's home-cooked meals."

Manuel ate out frequently. He wasn't into fast food, but was gaining weight nonetheless. Back then cultural fare in San Francisco was largely limited to Italian and Chinese. He had never learned how to cook, but found himself browsing the aisles of a grocery store with a list of familiar ingredients. Soon, he was teaching himself how to prepare his own version of his mother's recipes. He was a premed student at UC Berkeley, and around the same time he took a nutrition class. Soon he began to connect the dots between what he was doing in the kitchen and how he felt outside it. The more time he prepared his own meals, the better he felt: healthier, calmer, more in balance.

More than thirty years later, Villacorta is a leading nutrition expert and the author of several books on the subject. He offers these overarching guidelines to help reduce stress, enhance mood and optimize performance and health. Here are a few:

➤ **Eat whole.** Processed foods diminish our functioning. Over the long term, they can lead to fatigue, low metabolism and weight gain, all of which can impact mood and lead to inflammation, which we know is related to many chronic diseases. Villacorta's clients often believe, as I once did, that you can eat unhealthily so long as you are thin. He points out that you can be thin and have inflammation. Eliminate or reduce the amount of processed foods you consume, including foods laden with dyes, preservatives, sweeteners and other additives. Eat a greater variety of fruits, vegetables and whole grains. Opt for less frequent meat consumption, but choose higher-quality meats that have been grass fed and raised without hormones or antibiotics.

➤   **Take a longer view.** Villacorta defines a balanced diet as one that incorporates both macro- and micronutrients, derived from whole foods selected from various food groups. People can become very discouraged, even overwhelmed about their diets, because they fret over what they should be eating at every meal or snack. Villacorta observes that your body will not make day-to-day decisions. Think about your diet in terms of averages. Are you getting five servings of vegetables? If you did not consume enough vegetables today, have more tomorrow, so that over the course of a week you average out to five servings a day.

➤   **Think deeply and personally about balance.** A question that frequently comes up in Villacorta's work involves moderation and balance. "Moderation does not mean every day," he says. Balance is a soft objective that has to be determined with a very personal reference point. Maybe for you it means weekly or monthly. Maybe for you it means never, because your body can't handle a particular food. People have to cast a thoughtful and realistic eye upon what balance means for them and live accordingly.

From the Athletes' Playbook

The first thing Brandon Marcello did when he was hired as Stanford's director of sports performance in December 2007 was to completely disrupt the system. Marcello had beaten out two hundred other applicants vying for the opportunity to train the school's elite athletes, including a handful of Olympians, all of them masters in the most highly competitive sports in the world. Marcello, one of the country's top experts in athletic performance, brought with him big plans—plans that went beyond just the training—based on ideas that had been brewing in his head for some time.

In the field of sports, the focus had always been on developing the strength and conditioning of the athlete's body. But Marcello, who had worked with both college and professional athletes for close to two decades, felt intuitively that there was a lot more to the equation. He thought about the importance of every aspect of an athlete's life in achieving peak performance.

Midway through his career, Marcello went back to school for a PhD in what was considered then to be an odd field for someone who did what he did: nutrition. Fellow students asked why he was there, when many of them were trying to get a job doing what he had just left. Marcello was there on a hunch. Later, at Stanford, that hunch would be an important piece of the puzzle of optimal performance he would put together.

Few sports scientists were looking at nutrition as a core component of training back then. A few of Marcello's colleagues, early adopters, had begun to connect the dots. They talked among themselves about the link between nutrition and performance. "It's like staring at one side of the moon," he says, "and that's all you see—unaware of what the other side brings. But you just know there's something there, that it's all connected."

When Marcello arrived at the Farm, as Stanford is affectionately known, he reached out to the university community, tapping experts to collaborate on ways to improve the performance of the student athletes. He visited the sleep researchers. He knocked on the door of the psychologist experimenting with mindsets. He sought out experts studying the efficacy of mindfulness practices. Naturally he turned his attention to nutrition.

And he began to ask himself important questons. What if you could design a program that would use synergistic foods and nutrient combinations to support elite athletes in their quest to gain mastery over the physical and psychological stresses of extreme performance? Could you harness foods to support immunity, to support brain and mood performance, to address energy production, to reduce inflammation?

By 2011, in a collaboration between Stanford's athletic department and medical school and the Culinary Institute of America, the university launched its Performance Dining program in the first dining hall it had built on campus in twenty years. And Brandon Marcello, the draw-outside-the-lines guy with his hunch about nutrition and the importance of a 360-degree approach to the body, soon came to be known as one of the smartest guys in the strength and conditioning field.

Stanford's Performance Dining serves foods in six categories that impact both body and mind: enhanced immunity, anti-inflammatory components, food synergy, brain performance, sports performance and antioxidants. The program's overarching goal is to "serve synergistic food and nutrient combinations tailored to help students operate at their mental and physical peak at critical times." It emphasizes ten food categories that closely mirror our other nutritionists' recommendations: cruciferous vegetables (which include broccoli, kale, cauliflower, Brussels sprouts and other members of the cabbage family), whole grains, fish, red and purple fruits and vegetables, dark green vegetables, beans and legumes, reduced-fat milk products, nuts and seeds, extra virgin olive oil, and fresh herbs and spices.[107]

Healthy Eating Hack

If you are still unsure about the specifics of what you should be eating, you may want to use a technology-based healthy eating hack. There are a number of smartphone-based food apps on the market, including several you can use at the store as you shop to scan packaged food bar codes. Among these, I'm particularly partial to Fooducate, which grades food items on their healthiness and nutritional density based on an extraordinarily refined algorithm developed by experts. What I appreciate about Fooducate in particular is its simple and clear-eyed analysis of the devilry that often lies hidden in the small print of processed foods, including serving size, preservatives and additives, food colorings, and added sweeteners of all kinds. It also offers better alternatives.

It was when he had his own kids that Fooducate founder Hemi Weingarten went down the rabbit hole of the modern American diet. His son had just turned three and his twin daughters were one. Weingarten's wife came home from grocery shopping one day, and as he helped her unload the goods, the kids' yogurt caught his eyes. The box featured a cartoon character or two, but it was the yogurt he found interesting. It was super-bright

---

[107] For information on Performance Dining at Stanford, visit the Web site listed in Selected Sources.

pink and claimed to glow in the dark. Before that moment, Wein-garten had never before read an ingredient list or nutrition label. Somehow the neon yogurt served as a eureka moment. As he stared at the words GLOW IN THE DARK on that yogurt package, Hemi wondered what exactly he and his wife were putting in their children's mouths. And how was it going to affect them?

He had always loved food but had no particular interest in nutrition, although he considered himself a healthy person. He began to read voraciously about the modern food industry. He learned about the miracles of making obscenely cheap food, and the havoc that cheap food has wreaked on public health and emotional well-being.

The glow-in-the-dark yogurt tubes that had started all the trouble contained a dye called Red 40. The Food and Drug Ad-ministration (FDA) found the dye was perfectly fine to consume. But in Europe, Hemi learned, Red 40 was barely in use because some countries had banned it and others had required a warning label. The exact same product sold in the United States and in the United Kingdom contained Red 40 in the former and beet juice in the latter.

He dug further and found that some rat studies showed that the dye was a potential carcinogen, while other studies showed no harm. Yet other research showed that about one in ten chil-dren tended to be affected by artificial colors, including Red 40. Specifically, in some children the dye can lead to hyperactivity. Which was why Red 40 required a warning label in the UK.

"I said to myself, 'What is going on here? Are there other in-gredients I should be aware of?'"

The research was tough to come by; the science was often wildly contradictory; and some research appeared to be funded by food-industry-backed money. Distortions and smear cam-paigns seemed de rigueur. He thought there must be a better way

to find reliable information about what we are eating. His entre-
preneurial instinct began to sound an alarm. It was 2007 and
Steve Jobs had just announced the iPhone to much fanfare.
Within the year, Hemi had launched Fooducate.

For many people, eating healthy is about losing weight. But
the most important goal for Hemi is helping people make better
food choices amid the cacophony of misunderstanding, misinformation and distortion.

Practice

- **Eat with elegance.**
  Villacorta observes that during his initial assessments, some of his
  clients boast endlessly about their organic, preservative-free,
  locally sourced diets, but at the same time they admit to
  frequently eating on the go—standing up or while driving or
  walking. "I tell them, I don't care how organic your food is. You
  must take the time to eat mindfully," he says. He balances the
  importance of mindful eating with a dose of realism. He
  recommends that you choose one meal a day and eat it slowly
  while enjoying and observing the food and the surroundings, and
  the senses that arise in the body as you consume. "Get away from
  your desk and go out," he advises. "Chew slowly, eat purposefully
  and enjoy your meal."

- **Learn to eat slowly, deliberately and mindfully.**
  Jon Kabat-Zinn, the creator of the mindful-based stress reduction
  technique, designed the Mindful Eating Exercise (also known as
  the "Raisin Consciousness") to help give his clients a sensory
  experience of being mindful and fully present in their bodies, in

the here and now, as they eat. "When we taste with attention," Kabat-Zinn wrote in his book *Coming to Our Senses*, "even the simplest foods provide a universe of sensory experience, awakening us to them." The exercise involves eating a raisin slowly, deliberately and mindfully: examining it as if you have never seen it before by holding, seeing and touching it; smelling its aroma and the way that impacts your other senses; anticipating eating the raisin by placing it on your tongue, and leaving it there without chewing; tasting the raisin while chewing and observing the texture and flavors; and finally swallowing the raisin, observing details like the intention to ingest and the position the mouth takes. Take a crack at the raisin meditation. (Though you are welcome to do it with a simple food other than a raisin.)

Rule 9

Be Uncluttered

Out of clutter, find simplicity.

—ALBERT EINSTEIN

Leo Babauta's life changed in 2005. He was married and had a gaggle of children, including a couple of stepkids. He was overweight, a smoker. He was carrying a big load of debt. He couldn't make ends meet and was borrowing to put food on the table. He remembers being in a bad place, feeling stressed and overwhelmed by his inability to change his circumstances, no matter how hard he tried. At thirty-two, Leo found himself stuck firmly in the life he had made for himself.

What came next was born of desperation, of the realization that he couldn't change everything. So one day Leo decided that instead of changing everything, he would change one thing. Just one. He started with smoking. It was the one that bothered him the most, given the kids. He had tried to quit seven times before; all attempts ended in failure. He decided he would try again. This time he read everything he could find about change. He read about what worked and what didn't. He focused all his energy on quitting smoking. And that eighth time, he did it. Leo finally quit.

Next he set his sights on taking up running. "I was so out of shape," he remembers. "I couldn't even run for ten minutes. I had my doubts." He pushed forward anyway. For one month, he focused all his energy on running. In the first few weeks he found himself doing far more brisk walking than the slow trotting he liked to think of as running. Eventually, though, the scales tipped the other way. The trot turned into a solid jog. The jog became a steady run.

The next month, he tackled his diet. Then came clutter.

At the beginning of his fourth month of tackling the problem areas in his life, Leo took a look around. He was feeling hopeful, audacious even, and proud of his progress with smoking and getting in shape. But there was so much *stuff* everywhere. He wasn't sure how he had come by so much junk. It had crept into his life, he realized, a little bit at a time, from different sources, for all kinds of reasons. Bit by bit, it had added up to a mountain of anxiety. He remembers feeling inspired by writers who had written about simple living. The idea of paring down, of getting back down to the necessities appealed to Leo.

He started in the kitchen, focusing on one flat space at a time. He cleared out one counter, then another, then the dining room table, the floor. He looked for flat spaces—zones, he called them, clutter-free zones. He'd declutter and then he'd expand out.

The change was barely noticeable at first, he would recall later, but the shift in his space began to effect a colossal shift in his life. As his project gained momentum, it became clear to Leo that decluttering was less about getting rid of his stuff than about making room in his life for what was important: clearing the physical space to allow him the mental space to reflect on and do the things that were important to him. The results, he recalls, were exponential. And they were sublime.

A Revelation

Our second rule here involves becoming more conscious of how our physical space can impact our emotional space. Specifically, how clutter can affect stress levels.

When I began researching the relationship between clutter and the low-grade chronic stress in our lives, I experienced a kind of awakening. I'm no hoarder by any stretch and probably have what are fairly run-of-the-mill American pack-rat tendencies (as we all do to a lesser or greater degree). Suddenly, though, I became much more conscious of the toll that all the stuff in my life was taking. It was ever present, suffocating.

So I vowed to clear some clutter around the house before I sat down to write. Weeks passed and, try as I might, the piles remained like a pack of oblivious houseguests. For the first time, the same level of mess I had been living with became unbearable. Clutter, I decided, was the devil and the devil was trying to drown me—a slow death of mail, receipts, papers and magazines stacked on top of toys, clothes and shoes I don't wear, and other random objects. The objects and piles made it harder to think and process, and easier to lose patience, become angry and panic.

Graham, the bohemian drifter in the Steven Soderbergh film *Sex, Lies, and Videotape*, whom the script describes as "a man of obvious intelligence . . . only one key on his key ring," says: "Well, see, right now I have this one key, and I really like that. Everything I own is in my car. If I get an apartment, that's two keys. If I get a job, maybe I have to open and close once in a while—that's more keys. Or I buy some stuff and I'm worried about getting ripped off, so I get some locks and that's more keys. I just really like having the one key. It's clean, you know?"

Yes, Graham, we know. With our too many keys and too

much stuff, it feels to many of us as if we don't own any of it, but that it owns us. We are carrying it all on our back. It's there when we walk into our homes, when we sit down to think or write or read, create, or play with our kids—all the clutter is suffocating us.

Our relationship to "stuff" is closely related to our elusive quest for happiness. It feeds our need to quench the vague dissatisfaction that can sometimes underscore unconscious living. A great deal of our vices or addictions—shopping, food, alcohol or worse—stem from our unwillingness to be uncomfortable for long enough to diagnose the source of discomfort. And so we attempt to go over the discomfort, to go under it, to buy our way around it—anything but go through it.

Purchasing, acquiring, collecting and amassing has taken on a life of its own. It has become a sport (*Black Friday!*), a form of peer pressure (*You know you want it*), a mark of status (*The true definition of luxury—yours*), even an ego stroke (*You deserve it*). We are addicted to the temporary fix of shopping and if we were to give it up, what would we do instead? How would we soothe ourselves?

Clutter—and its pathological first cousin, hoarding—is big business, the subject of countless products, stores, reality shows, Web sites and articles. We are endlessly obsessed with buying and collecting stuff as an end in itself, but then we turn around and also purchase to conquer the resulting chaos—madness, when you think about it!

Mikael Cho, founder of the Web site pickcrew.com, was a project manager at a design agency when he felt his brain "becoming polluted by so many things, both physical and digital" that he couldn't get much work done. In the mornings, he says, he felt fresh, but as the day wore on, his anxiety levels would spike and the streams of clutter slowed his work to a near-halt.

This research brought him to what scientists have known for

a while: Our stress hormones spike when we are dealing with our possessions. Physical clutter impedes our ability to focus and process information, even when it's out of sight. It competes for our attention, decreases performance and increases stress.[108] The effects are similar to multitasking, which results in sensory overload.[109]

And, Cho further discovered, overconsumption of digital material has a similar effect. The digital miscellany in our lives—the files, the apps, the pings, the dings, the lights, the blinks and the winks of social media notifications and smartphones—competes for our attention. They form a digital clutter, creating a low-grade but chronic form of stress that lessens our ability to live in the present and with purpose.[110] "When you have to-do items constantly floating around in your head or you hear a ping or vibrate every few minutes, your brain doesn't get a chance to fully enter creative flow or to process experiences," writes Cho.

With Cho's findings and cautions in mind, I sought to enlist the help of a mentor, someone whose organization I could perhaps model. I turned to my friend Toiya, a political activist and the mother of two young boys—and also one of the most ordered people I have ever known. Toiya's organization and efficiency are just astounding. Her counters are so consistently clutter-free, a few of us have taken to joking that magical creatures would appear, remove offending debris and disappear again.

---

[108] Mikael Cho, "How Clutter Affects Your Brain (and What You Can Do About It)," *Lifehacker*, July 5, 2013.

[109] See Stephanie McMains and Sabine Kastner, "Interactions of Top-Down and Bottom-Up Mechanisms in Human Visual Cortex," *The Journal of Neuroscience*, January 12, 2011.

[110] "Bits are a new material," wrote Mark Hurst, author of *Bit Literacy*, on controlling the flow of information in the digital age, quoted in Mikael Cho, "How Clutter Affects Your Brain (and What You Can Do About It)."

"How are you so organized?" I asked Toiya.

"That's just what you can see," she told me. "If you were to look in my closets and dresser drawers, they are a nightmare."

I felt oddly let down, but it was a moment of clarity. I then saw clutter as a metaphor for our lives: The appearance of order on the outside. Chaos on the inside. The sequestered chaos splitting at the seams and threatening to engulf us, inside and out.

And there's another stress-inducing cost to clutter: the simple dollar price of overconsumption. It's not just that we're drowning in stuff we don't need; we're paying for it with money we don't have. In poll after poll, Americans say that the state of their finances is one of the biggest sources of their stress. Yet over the past two decades, consumer spending—which accounts for roughly two-thirds of our economy—has been fueled largely by debt, with savings being negligible, if existent at all. "That kind of spending is unsustainable economically, environmentally or spiritually," author Tony Wagner told me.

The Compulsion

All the decluttering tips in the world will not help us until we understand the compulsion to accumulate things we don't need in the first place. Our clutter-free hero Babauta, now the author of Zen Habits, a wildly successful blog about his experiment with simple living, as well as a book, *The Power of Less*, helps us grasp this problem.

The proclivity toward clutter, Babauta explains, comes from two main emotional motivations. You either fear the future or are attached to the past. Fear of the future: You're holding on to things because you think you *might* need them later. Attachment to the past: You can't part with the physical representation, the mementos of the great things you've done in your life—things that make you feel loved or good about yourself.

The idea of attachment to the past made immediate sense to me. I decided to blame my own clutter on the Ayatollah.

Some part of me suspected that the perpetual disarray in my surroundings was somehow related to the chaos that had lingered within, ever since I fled the Iranian Revolution as a child. I had, for instance, squirreled away scores of photographs and random mementos of my two children's baby years. Was this because all of mine were left behind in the urgency of flight?

But any good feelings I may have derived from the material things I had collected over the years had long been replaced by the dread of their growing presence in my life. Where I once cohabitated with clutter quite nicely, my body and mind began to tolerate their leaden weight less and less. The tokens of the past felt more and more like anchors.

In the end, mindfulness took precedence. I was desperate for greater clarity and greater peace. And in order to get it, I had to confront the demons. I had to declutter.

I began one day, and continued the next. And for a few minutes or hours every day for months. I am still decluttering. It is a work in progress. But I finally understood what Babauta meant. The ever-present sense of overwhelm receded. There were, suddenly, wide-open spaces, both outside and in.

The Way Forward

Our human tendency is to run toward positive emotions—security, pleasure, happiness, joy, bliss—and to do our best to avoid negative ones. Our consumerist culture, echoed throughout the media, celebrates the material as a means toward such positive goals.[111] In fact, it has become an *addiction*. But the addiction is not so much to buying stuff, but trying to attain that joy and pleasure we associate with consumption. The material items we buy to capture fleetingly the relief and pleasure only serve to further compound our stress over time. It is unsustainable from both a personal and a global perspective.

Look around you. Does all that stuff bring you anything positive? Or are you just left with a mountain of meaningless things— along, perhaps, with debt?

Nothing you can buy will replace conscious living and presence. True joy can only come from an inner state of being. Not from being attached to the past. Not from being fearful of the future. Only in remaining firmly rooted in the present moment.

How, then, can we embark upon clearing the clutter—both mental and physical?

➤ **Tackle one flat surface at a time.** If you're feeling moved to undertake a frenzy of purging, don't. Start with small steps. One surface, one shelf, the floor of a closet . . .

➤ **Find a place for each thing you want to keep in your life.** Keep the things you need or love dearly, and give them a meaningful physical place. Everything else should go.

➤ **Become conscious of bringing things in to begin with.** If you're in a hole, stop digging. If you are drowning in piles, stop adding to them. Be conscious of your spending. Set a period of time for a

---

[111] Ryan Rigoli, San Francisco–based entrepreneur and leadership coach.

spending freeze—say, a week or a month with no purchases other than groceries and the bare essentials.

➤ **Figure out your triggers.** Consider journaling as a way of becoming aware of what's happening—thought and behavior habits and patterns that trigger unwanted results. The next time you feel the urge to buy, write down what you think the item will add to your life and reflect on the real needs you're seeking to fill.

➤ **Get another perspective.** Consider the many blind spots and shadow spots that may keep you constrained. Get the counsel of someone , you trust—someone who can look at you objectively. And then listen and be open to feedback.

Find Your Own Balance

Los Angeles psychologist Amelia Ramirez was once invited by a new friend to "a very simple dinner." The invitation came with a disclaimer: "I don't have a couch. I don't have any furniture. I don't have anything!"

Ramirez was okay with that.

When she arrived at the woman's house, she found that there were amazingly few pieces of furniture. Aside from a bed, there were two tables: one with a computer on it in the living room, and another with a printer in the kitchen.

Ramirez perched atop her host's kitchen counter and watched her prepare green beans, chard and broccoli. Then she placed them into a big boiling pan—one of two pans the woman owned.

Once dinner was ready, they sat down at the "table," a cardboard box in the living room.

"She brought the bowl of mixed greens and a bag full of nori seaweed, with homemade organic hot sauce to the box/table," Ramirez recalled. "And we sat there and dined in the most elegant way I had in a while."

They discussed meditation, work, healing and love.

"It was enchanting. My dinner companion was mesmerizing," observed Ramirez. She was impressed by the woman's simplicity, and how her having "nothing" meant that she had so much more than things. She was freed to focus on what she really cared about.

The woman was missing so many of the things that clutter our lives, but she was brimming with vitality and enthusiasm. "She was vibrant and very, very alive," noted Ramirez. "And perhaps her lack of stuff gave her space and freedom. It certainly made me want less. I left thinking the woman was one of the richest women I had ever met."

Such extreme minimalism may not suit you, but hopefully the message has some appeal. Chaos distracts us and restricts our creativity and productivity. And although some people might even need a certain degree of clutter in order to be productive, the important thing is to seek and find your own balance.

Begin Practicing

Our whole life is practice. Anything you do over and over again is practice, and soon becomes habit. Consciously or unconsciously, we are practicing what we do all the time—whether for good or for ill. Leo Babauta echoes this principle with a quote by Aristotle: "We are what we repeatedly do. Excellence, then, is not an act but a habit." Our habits can make or break us, so it is important to look at your current behavior deliberately and see whether you need to find ways to create new ones.

There is no quick fix for habits, though. The clutter in your life is the physical manifestation of habits that have built up over years, so it would be a mistake to think you can change your life overnight.

At the end of his year of decluttering, Babauta took stock. "Looking back on it," he says, "my list of things I transformed about my life sounds remarkable. But I changed slowly." With time and patience, he was rewarded with a new perspective on life. "You wouldn't have even recognized me back then. It's like I was someone else entirely."

Practice

- **Declutter, slowly.**

  Select the room you spend the most time in and, over the course of a week, spend fifteen minutes each day removing clutter from one surface at a time. After each session, remain mindful of how you relate to the newly cleared space. If you are so inclined, write about your feelings and observations. The decluttering might even make you anxious or stressed at first. That's okay. Write about those feelings too, consider where they may be coming from—and then try to release them.

CHAPTER NINE

World, Mind and Body

Our deepest fear is not that we are inadequate. Our deepest fear is that we are powerful beyond measure. It is our light, not our darkness, that most frightens us. . . . Your playing small does not serve the world. There is nothing enlightened about shrinking so that other people will not feel insecure around you. We are all meant to shine, as children do. We were born to make manifest the glory of God that is within us. It is not just in some of us; it is in everyone, and as we let our own light shine, we unconsciously give others permission to do the same. As we are liberated from our own fear, our presence automatically liberates others.

—MARIANNE WILLIAMSON

Rule 10

Be Present

You need not leave your room.

Remain sitting at your table and listen.

You need not even listen, simply wait.

You need not even wait, just learn to become quiet, and still, and solitary.

The world will freely offer itself to you to be unmasked.

It has no choice; it will roll in ecstasy at your feet.

—FRANZ KAFKA

"Meditation is not a priority," complained the caller to the radio program. "Food is a priority. Water is a priority. And shelter. Not meditation."

Bob Roth, head of the David Lynch Foundation, was being interviewed—along with a representative from UNICEF—about his organization's mission to bring meditation to traumatized populations, including refugee camps in the Middle East and schools in some of Chicago's toughest, most crime-ridden neighborhoods.

The criticism was one he heard often in those early days in 2005 as he and director David Lynch set out to establish the organization.

Meditation is nice, he was told, but not essential. Certainly not a matter of survival.

"How about spending that good money on books, classrooms or better teachers?" asked another caller.

Roth knew early on that one of the foundation's most important tasks would be to educate people about the social epidemic of toxic stress and trauma.

"Dealing with toxic stress," he says, "is not a luxury. So many scientists have now come out to confirm that, but the writing was on the wall even back then. Stress is widely considered the number one health epidemic of our time. Modern medicine can't prevent it. There is no pill to cure it."

Bob Roth does not believe in false dichotomies. Yes, he says, books, food, water and shelter are absolutely essential, but so is learning how to heal the nightmare of trauma and stress that incapacitates many of our children and stunts their healing and learning processes—the stress, in fact, that impedes progress in our at-risk communities. Dealing with stress is akin to teaching a man how to fish. It's a long-term investment in rebuilding for the future.

Research shows that meditation does not just heal the brain; it also wakes up learning centers within the brain. The meditator learns not just to manage his stress, but builds a greater resilience for the inevitable stress that comes his way. Roth's mission—and that of the foundation—is to provide vulnerable populations throughout the world with a tool they can learn in a few hours and use for the rest of their lives.

Roth began meditating when he was eighteen years old, not long after Bobby Kennedy's assassination. Kennedy's death was a devastating blow. Raised in an intensely political family in the Bay Area—"I knew I was a Democrat before I knew I was Jewish!"—he fell into a deep depression.

It was a time of social and political discord in Berkeley, where Roth lived. "There were tanks parked outside our doors and I was lost. I had wanted to be a senator like Kennedy. I wanted to change the world." The stress was overwhelming, and some days depression threatened to engulf him.

Someone Roth respected suggested that he try transcendental meditation, assuring him it would help him handle the stress. "I said, 'I'm a doer. I'm not a reflective person. And I'm Jewish!' But my friend was adamant, so I went to the lecture." A skeptical man by nature, at the lecture he asked: "How much do I have to believe for meditation to work?"

Not at all, the speaker said.

Two days after he learned to meditate, Roth realized he was onto something.

"The focus and clarity were profound," he recalls. As for the stress and despair he had been experiencing: "It was as if the fog had lifted."

The Transformative Power of Mindfulness

I found my way to the trend of meditating lawyers almost by accident: I happened to meet Barbara in a parking lot. As we chatted, she told me she was in the throes of a merger. What puzzled me was how centered she seemed, exuding a calm, joyful energy. As a recovering attorney who'd escaped the law because the stress had tied me in knots, I was intrigued.

When I made that observation to her, she told me she had a longtime yoga practice, which she had begun in college and continued while she was a law student at the University of Chicago. Over the years, the yoga evolved into a meditation practice. Barbara had also attended a slew of continuing legal education courses that incorporated elements of meditation and mindfulness. Meditation, she said, helped her practice law in a way that shuts out a lot of the static, the noise, the irrelevant.

I reached out to an old law school friend later that day. "What are lawyers doing to alleviate stress these days?" I asked her.

"Does scratching my eyes out count as a stress reliever?" she asked.

"Well, no," I replied. "It's quite the opposite, really."

"That's all I know." She shrugged.

In all my years in the legal profession, I met scores of attorneys who felt as my old friend did—and almost none like Barbara. Most attorneys accept that misery is implicit in their trade. The professors had virtually taught us that in law school. Statistics certainly bear that out: A well-known Johns Hopkins study found that lawyers are more prone to depression than members of any other profession. According to the American Bar Association, as many as 20 percent of American lawyers abuse alcohol or other substances. And an often-cited study by the National Institute for Occupational Safety and Health conducted two decades ago found that male lawyers between the ages of twenty and sixty-four are more than twice as likely to die from suicide than their counterparts in other occupations. In a 2011 article entitled "The Depressed Lawyer," Washington, DC, psychologist Tyger Latham who had treated more than his fair share of lawyers asked: "Why are so many lawyers so unhappy?"[112]

Once I began to dig a bit further, a different picture began to emerge. Barbara, the ethereal lawyer from the parking lot, turned out not to be such an anomaly, but part of a growing nationwide trend transforming the landscape of the law. The earliest organized meditation retreat for lawyers was held in October 1998

---

[112] Tyger Latham, "The Depressed Lawyer," *Psychology Today*, May 2, 2011.

for Yale law students and faculty. Since then, mindfulness practices have popped up with increasing frequency—from national
conferences on mindful lawyering to courses in law schools
(CUNY and the University of Miami, among them) to retreats
for trial lawyers, workshops for judges, and continuing legal education for practicing attorneys at Zen and Buddhist centers.

Growing numbers of attorneys are embracing some form of
practice to achieve mindfulness. Their reasons for doing so are
varied, but chief among them are stress management and improved mental and physical health—benefits backed by many research findings from scientists at Harvard and the University of
Pennsylvania, among others. In one study, Harvard researchers
found that practicing a form of mindful meditation for as little as
thirty minutes a day for eight weeks resulted in measurable changes
in the brain regions involved in learning, memory, emotion regulation and stress.

The growing openness to the practice of mindfulness arose
out of high levels of stress associated with the legal profession
and the overwhelming cost it can impose on the lives of many.[113]
In the long run, however, the practice also benefited attorneys in
other ways. It made them more skilled and effective at work, more
focused, more active listeners, better at helping clients—and all
this progress came in a way that was sustainable.

The mindfulness movement has already served as an important foundation for some innovations in the law, including "collaborative law," a less acrimonious, downright enlightened alternative
to a typical divorce (troubleshoot and problem solve, rather than
fight to win), and "restorative justice," a criminal law approach
that emphasizes reconciliation, restoration, healing and rehabili-

---

[113] Trailblazing public interest lawyer and law professor Charles Halpern is one of
those at the forefront of the movement.

tation.[114] The growing inclination among attorneys to rethink some of the more traditional aspects of law practice are making way for the emergence of law as a healing profession and lawyers as peacemakers—something that, frankly, may seem downright blasphemous to most.

A Place at the Table

It may have seemed tempting not too long ago to dismiss mindfulness and meditation as a hippy-dippy endeavor, but those views have been increasingly challenged and overwhelmed by science. Meditation and other contemplative practices are continuing to claim their place at the table of mainstream medicine. This is true for a variety of reasons—chief among them, the recognition that hordes of us are overwheled, that toxic stress wreaks havoc upon our bodies, and that the practice of meditation has significant and measurable stress reduction properties.

Hundreds of studies validate the health benefits of mindfulness training. The range is extensive: from strengthening the immune system and relieving chronic pain to thickening the brain's cortex, lowering blood pressure and even healing psoriasis.[115] Not just beneficial to adults, mindfulness also increases children's self-esteem and boosts school performance by improving their ability to ignore distractions and concentrate better, observes writer Judith Woods. It has even been advanced as a means of addressing attention deficit disorders.

Recall the study about loneliness among the elderly popula-

---

[114] Doug Chermak, environmental lawyer and director of the law program at the Center for Contemplative Mind in Society.

[115] David Hochman, "Mindfulness: Getting Its Share of Attention," *New York Times*, November 1, 2013.

tion conducted by scientist David Creswell that proved a mindful-based stress reduction program not only decreased participants' sense of loneliness, but also significantly reduced proinflammatory gene expression and C-reactive protein in their blood. Meditation's ability to lower inflammation levels is particularly important because inflammation plays a significant role in chronic disease. And while the study did not assess whether meditation also helps to directly reduce the occurrence of disease, the possibilities are significant and far-reaching.[116]

Rooted in the East

Mindfulness is rooted in Eastern faiths, most prominently Buddhism, where the Buddha described the "direct path to enlightenment." Consider this remarkable passage from the much more recent Baha'i writings:

> Meditation is the key for opening the doors of mysteries. In that state man abstracts himself: in that state man withdraws himself from all outside objects; in that subjective mood he is immersed in the ocean of spiritual life and can unfold the secrets of things-in-themselves . . . This faculty brings forth from the invisible plane the sciences and arts. Through the meditative faculty inventions are made possible, colossal undertakings are carried out; through it governments can run smoothly.

---

[116] Dr. Creswell's study made explicit use of the mindfulness-based meditation technique. When asked if other forms of contemplative practice provided similar benefits, he observed that we don't have the data to indicate whether or not there is something distinct about mindfulness-based stress reduction techniques; however, he suspected that having a formal meditation program with a teacher is beneficial because it provides structure and helps train and build skills.

Mindfulness is not just transforming lawyers and the practice of law. Once you begin looking for it, you will find that it has begun to pervade (and enhance) our lives in the most unexpected ways. Athletes use it to achieve better outcomes. The U.S. military, as we discovered in Rule 1, offers it to soldiers to help promote resilience. Mindfulness training has become commonplace in both creative industries and many Silicon Valley companies. Google famously offers a frequently sold-out seven-week mindfulness class led by veteran engineer Chade-Meng Tan (whose official job title is Jolly Good Fellow). Mindfulness and meditation feature strongly in Arianna Huffington's Third Metric, which seeks to create a new way to thrive and measure success. The principles are also taught at legion elite universities. In sports, on university campuses, in hospitals, public schools, government offices—the list goes on and on—mindfulness is touted as the key to evolution.[117]

Despite its increasing presence, I find that in the course of lectures and seminars, participants ask with a slightly embarrassed air: What exactly is mindfulness? How do I go about being present?

The idea can be elusive, in part because its explanation seems so deceptively simple.

Mindfulness is your intent to bring awareness to the present moment, both inside and out. It means, in essence, deliberately paying full attention to what is happening around you and within you—in your body, heart and mind. It is awareness without criticism, so that we may observe and clear our thoughts, without judgment, as they pass. That is, noticing our thoughts and our bodily sensations without labeling them or judging them.

As a brain-training technique, mindfulness helps us shut out

[117] David Hochman, "Mindfulness: Getting Its Share of Attention," *The New York Times*, November 1, 2013. David Derbyshire, "Should We Be Mindful of Mindfulness," *The Guardian*, February 23, 2014.

the buzz and achieve mental clarity. It is not "zoning out," writes Deepak Chopra, but rather zoning in, that serves as a "cognitive decluttering." It also provides a deeper quality of rest than sleep, as seen through EEG measurements of brain hormone levels in the blood and cellular metabolism.[118]

Many are put off by the very fluidity of form associated with mindfulness, which can seem too ethereal for our bean-counting brains that crave both hard boundaries and incessant, mindless chatter. The reality, though, is that the practice of mindfulness comes in myriad forms. The classic pose is widely known: a person sitting cross-legged, with eyes closed, shoulders and jaw relaxed, and breathing deep with special attention focused on the air being drawn into the body and then exhaled. However, there are as many ways to practice mindfulness as there are human beings on this planet. There is the walking meditation described by the mystic Thich Nhat Hanh: "Walk as if you are kissing the earth with your feet." The mindful spending meditation by Zen teacher and physician Jan Chozen Bays is featured in Rule 6.

Director and actor Kenneth Branagh began meditating at the incessant urging of a friend during a particularly dark period of his life. He said of the experience: "I immediately found meditation maddening. It was silly, pointless, a waste of time. But toward the end of the thirty minutes, for a brief moment I experienced simple, weightless happiness. I wasn't thinking about anything at all. The mental chatter had disappeared. Afterward I felt as if I had just returned from a holiday. And with that, my life changed forever, because I had found a way to still my mind."[119]

---

[118] Deepak Chopra, "Sleep and Meditation," www.deepakchopra.com/blog/view /1613/sleep_and_meditation.

[119] "Kenneth Branagh's Aha! Moment: How I Learned to Meditate," *O, The Oprah Magazine*, May 2011.

Meditation (or Something Like It) on the High Court

I had it on good authority (Google) that one of the country's lawyers-in-chief, Supreme Court Justice Stephen Breyer, was a "big meditator" and so a few e-mails and telephone calls later, I found myself channeling my best Oprah on the other end of a telephone line with Justice Breyer, asking in what may have been a slightly overdramatic tone: "How, sir, did you first arrive at your meditation practice?"

He paused for an instant before his elegant baritone boomed through the phone line: "To say that I am a meditator is overstating it," he said. "I don't know that what I do is meditation, or even whether it has a name. For ten or fifteen minutes twice a day I sit peacefully. I relax and think about nothing, or as little as possible. And that is what I've done for a couple of years."

But wait! I thought. Isn't that the definition of meditation?

He continued: "And really, I started because it's good for my health. My wife said this would be good for my blood pressure and she was right. It really works. I read once that the practice of law is like attempting to drink water from a fire hose. And if you are under stress, meditation—or whatever you choose to call it—helps. Very often I find myself in circumstances that may be considered stressful—say, in oral arguments where I have to concentrate very hard for extended periods. If I come back at lunchtime, I sit for fifteen minutes and perhaps another fifteen minutes later. Doing this makes me feel more peaceful, focused and better able to do my work."

It was not until later that I grasped the full wisdom of what Justice Breyer had told me. It doesn't matter what your meditation or mindfulness practice looks like, where and how you do it, what you choose to call it—or whether you choose to call it anything at all. You will reap the benefits regardless.

This echoed the words of David Lynch Foundation executive director Bob Roth: "How much do I have to believe for meditation to work?" he had asked. Not at all, said the speaker.

Greater Power over Stressful Circumstances

Bill Resnick struggled in his teens and early twenties with depression, substance abuse and alcoholism. At twenty-two he got sober. He had been in psychotherapy for years and found it helpful. Eventually he attended medical school to become a psychiatrist. In the course of his training, while teaching at a clinic focused on evidence-based interpersonal psychotherapies, he began studying the scientific evidence that mindfulness practices work for major depression. His interest was piqued, but he wouldn't pursue it until he read *The Wise Heart*, a book about meditation by Jack Kornfield, a renowned psychologist and meditation teacher who had also trained as a Buddhist monk. Resnick appreciated the wisdom, especially since he was struggling in a ten-year relationship that was on its last leg. On a whim, he took an introductory six-week meditation class. He began with a very simple practice. The teacher encouraged Resnick and his group to meditate for five minutes a day during the first week. During the second week, they increased the time to ten minutes. Resnick found it so useful, he began to do twenty minutes every day.

Through his mindfulness practice, he found a path that helped him look at himself in a very different way than he had in therapy. He recalls, "Mindfulness gave me a greater sense of power over my stress and discomfort. It also helped me to take personal inventory and acknowledge when I was wrong in a situation. It allowed me to dissect my resentments during stressful and chaotic situations."

Even now he sometimes falls back into resentments, but the difference is that there is a continuous presence, a subtle awareness, of what's happening early on. It allows him not to become fully embroiled in the circumstances unfolding around him, letting him shift his perception quickly and focus on solutions. The typical practice is about focusing on the sensation of breathing and what's happening in the present moment. The mind wanders, but it's also interesting to notice how busy the mind can get.

While very simple, mindfulness practice is anything but easy. Just being present and paying attention to the moment is a straightforward, elegant instruction—and surprisingly difficult to accomplish. "Even if you've done it for a while, it requires effort and commitment to maintain," Resnick observes.

It is a mistaken notion that meditation is about having a blank mind. The goal of meditation is to slowly quiet the mind, to allow the mind to be as it is, to be able to witness it and not be attached to it and its stories. A big part of the benefit of mindfulness for Resnick has been not having to react to the many daily stress triggers: noticing your internal response rather than automatically reacting, recognizing the emotions and even appreciating them, witnessing the emotions that arise, experiencing them, "being with them," and consciously not tightening around them. He began to embrace the discomfort of those moments, staying in them and moving through them. The practice of mindfulness, says Resnick, is about practicing *acceptance*.

A year or so after he began his meditation practice, one of Resnick's friends talked him into attending a mostly silent meditation retreat for five days. He wasn't sure what to expect, but was amused by how, even at a place with very little stimulation, his mind could still chatter away and find things to obsess about. His job at one retreat was to clean the bathrooms. "It was hilarious how much I obsessed about cleaning the bathrooms. People don't like being alone with themselves or with their minds without distraction. If you pull that apart, it's very interesting."

By the end of the five days, he experienced a quality of joy, lightness and awakening that he had not expected. He recalls it as a very distinct ability to be in the moment without the need for stimulation or clinging.

That radical sense of presence slowly faded upon his return to real life, but what remained was the realization that it was possible. And it changed him in other, subtle ways. He found he needed less stimulation—or perhaps it was that he just didn't seek as much. On his way to the gym or during a run, he used to listen to music. Now he took advantage of the moment. He walked, he listened, he paid attention to what was happening around him.

When Resnick facilitates mindfulness groups, people will sometimes come up to him and say, "I can't meditate." Bill chuckles and says, "It's like saying, 'I can't play the piano,' without ever taking a class. You have to start from where you are."

Resnick has been sober for almost twenty-seven years now, a psychiatrist for almost twenty. Among the many lessons he has learned in his journey, two stand out. First, so much of our serenity is in our attitude, he says. It's an inside job. Second, spiritual growth is not like getting a degree—it's not as if you do it once and then you're forever done with school. You have to constantly work at it or you will fall into old habits. You can have a wonderful heightened awareness and be awakened one moment to what's in front of you. And then you can fall back again. You keep at it. Day to day, hour to hour, moment to moment. And third, even in the most dire of circumstances, we can *choose* how we respond. That is perhaps the greatest benefit of a mindfulness practice: it helps us to observe the reactions that emerge—helps us notice, but not get pulled into, negative thoughts. It helps with how we perceive the stories, and how we react to them.

"Part of the accepting and allowing the present moment is paying attention to the body and its many sensations," he says. "And allowing a softening around the discomfort, but being gentle with that. I have witnessed people going through a great deal of distress transform in the moment. That doesn't mean that they're cured for the rest of their lives, but it is immensely healing."

Resnick recalls a favorite passage from Kornfield's *The Wise Heart*: "It's like two arrows, the Buddha said. The first arrow is the initial event itself, the painful experience. It has happened; we cannot avoid it. The second arrow is the one we shoot into ourselves. This arrow is optional. We can add to the initial pain a contracted, angry, rigid, frightened state of mind. Or we can learn to experience the same painful event with less identification and aversion, with a relaxed and compassionate heart."

Practice

- **Meditate (quickly).**
  Martin Boroson, author of *One-Moment Meditation*, suggests beginning a meditation practice with a single minute.[120] The idea is not to learn to meditate for a long time, but quickly. You can

---

[120] You can find Boroson's short video on how to meditate in a moment at: www .youtube.com/watch?v=F6eFFCi12v8.

make a meaningful change in your state of mind in a single moment. Begin by setting a timer for just one minute and then following fairly typical meditation instructions: Close your eyes or lower your gaze; put your body in a balanced, stable position; and simply focus on your breathing for a full minute. It's common to face distraction and your mind may meander even in that minute. But that doesn't mean you're failing. The important thing is to get your mind back to breathing and not to judge yourself. After a minute, he observes, you will notice a shift in your state of mind toward greater peace. Boroson's philosophy is that it doesn't matter that you won't experience total enlightenment in that minute. If you can just turn the volume down a little bit on the uncontrolled thoughts in your mind, that's useful.

- **Access, feel and release negative emotions.**
Ryan Rigoli is a gifted life and leadership coach, and cofounder of Soulful Brand. He works with clients who become stuck in unhealthy or even destructive narratives, making it challenging for them to flourish. According to Rigoli, a person can have different motivations—some conscious, others unconscious—that are at odds with one another. He helps resolve these conflicts in exercises during sessions or through journaling. Just the act of acknowledging and hearing the different parts speak can be dramatic and life changing. Sometimes people don't need solutions. They just need to be heard; the emotions they feel need to be accessed, felt and released. Try the following exercise that Rigoli does with his clients:

Every emotion has a physical sensation connected to it. During stressful periods, identify the emotion and the associated physical symptom—for example, a tight chest or cramp in the stomach.

  o Focus your attention on the site of the symptom.

○ Place your hand on that spot and focus your energy on the symptom and attempt to feel the emotion more deeply.

○ Take deep breaths and envision the breath directing toward the site of the physical symptom.

○ Continue to breathe deeply.

If you allow yourself to feel the full charge of the negative emotion in the moment, you will find that the emotion often dissipates.

■ **Use Mindfulness as the Entry Point for Your Breaks and Buffers**
Jon Kabat-Zinn has defined mindfulness as "the awareness that arises through paying attention; on purpose in the present moment, and nonjudgmentally."

Together, these three elements of mindfulness—finding awareness through paying attention; discovering purpose in the present; and accepting without judgment—make up the entry points for the conscious breaks and buffers that we all need to introduce into our everyday lives to help downgrade feelings of stress and overwhelm, as well as to create constructive, meaningful narratives of challenges, big and small.

In Appendix I, I have supplied a solid list of strategies, of possible breaks and buffers, to help relieve or downgrade feelings of stress and overwhelm.

Pick any of the strategies listed in Appendix I or choose one of your own, and practice Kabat-Zinn's three elements of mindfulness as you take part in the activity.

○ If you have decided to go for a walk in nature, for example, pay attention as you take each step.

○ Observe your surroundings.

- Feel the sensation of the air or wind against your skin.

- Tune into the sounds of your steps.

- Keep mind on the present and as thoughts rise up, observe and acknowledge them and, without judgment, let them pass.

- Through it all, continue to return to your breath. "Feelings come and go like clouds in a windy sky. Conscious breathing is my anchor," writes famed Zen master Thich Nhat Hanh. "Breathing in, I calm body and mind. Breathing out, I smile. Dwelling in the present moment I know this is the only moment."

- Commit to taking part in this practice, alongside any activity that appeals to you, at least once a day.

- Begin with five minutes, if you find it difficult to go longer.

- Slowly extend the activity to twenty minutes or more, twice a day. Or continue to practice for just five minutes, multiple times a day.

In the End: Be

An Afterword

We shall not cease from exploration, and the end of all our exploring will be to arrive where we started and know the place for the first time.

—T. S. ELIOT

When one is released from the prison of self, that is indeed freedom! For self is the greatest prison. When this release takes place, one can never be imprisoned. Unless one accepts dire vicissitudes, not with dull resignation, but with radiant acquiescence, one cannot attain this freedom.

—ABDU'L-BAHÁ

On the day of the historic People's March for action on climate change in New York City this past September, I was asked to give a talk in Los Angeles about environmental sustainability. A few days before my presentation, I sat down to sift through my research and materials in order to create a handful of PowerPoint slides.

Later, as I reviewed the narrative reflected in the slides, I was struck by how closely the story of environmental sustainability mirrors the story of stress: the sense of denial in some, and alarm and overwhelm in others; the questioning of the culture and institutions we have always taken for granted; the need to find novel and creative solutions, the importance of crafting new and better narratives; the need for collaboration and community.

Stress, by all indications, is the tale of personal sustainability. That is, our everyday habits and practices must be sustainable for us as individuals. They must be sustainable for our families, communities, nations and planet.

"To make progress," writes neuroscientist Tali Sharot, "we need to imagine alternative realities—better ones—and we need to believe we can achieve them." Tech entrepreneur Peter Thiel, who has created several wildly successful companies including PayPal, knows a thing or two about alternative realities and how to achieve them. He often makes the distinction between indefinite optimists—people with a bullish view of the future, but with no plan as to how to make that happen—and definite optimists—those who have both a vision of the future and a plan for bringing it about.

How to join the ranks of the latter? I am a big believer in reverse engineering.

A trove of new and old writings about stress and authentic happiness provide directions to the new realities we seek. These writings tell us that the state of our world, our minds and our bodies will determine how successful we will be in our quest.

The way we experience stress is a function of a great many things—foremost among them, of the stories we choose to tell ourselves about stress. This is the singular power of perception: the power to imagine and create our world, to derive meaning from the bliss and the suffering that marks every human being's life.

Many of our culture's current definitions of success and happiness revolve around the self—measuring value and worth through power and status, looks and luxury. But the weight of scientific and other literature makes clear that a compass calibrated for authentic success and happiness is focused outward: to purpose, giving and kindness. We must realign our materialistic definitions— changing our minds where necessary—to reflect the fact that lasting happiness comes from a life of purpose and service.

The need for harmony, balance and moderation also extends to our bodies and dwelling places. Clearing junk from our bodies and physical environments makes us stronger, more creative, more focused. "Amazingly," writes author Ingrid Collins, "when we change something on a physical plane, we also seem to change it in the spiritual dimension."

One common thread weaving through these three gateways— world, mind and body—is mindfulness and presence: consciousness, in the moment, of our thoughts, actions and reactions. Another is community, camaraderie and belonging: our most vital protective factors during times of adversity. A third is the willingness to become comfortable with discomfort and uncertainty, to dare to challenge current realities and imagine new ones that may be vastly different from those that have come before.

All these are themes as old as humans and faith, and yet also fresh and new in the way science continues to validate and elucidate their place and practice in our lives.

We began this book looking to relieve stress. We are ending it looking to understand and embrace stress, to use it as a measure of progress or the lack thereof, with a deeper understanding of the Zen proverb: "The obstacle in the path becomes the path." Perhaps, too, we find ourselves armed with a better road map to what many are calling a new age, different forms of thinking, a new approach to life.

Here is the road to serenity, to a life of purpose, empathy, creativity and bliss.

APPENDIX I

BREAKS, BUFFERS AND PROTECTIVE FACTORS: A LIGHTNING ROUND OF PROVEN STRATEGIES

We know by now that stress has many potential upsides and that our perception of stress is key to its impact on us, but it is important that we continue to find ways to avoid the toxic impacts of chronic stress by interspersing periods of acute stress with periods of low or no stress.

According to James Gross, a top expert on emotions and emotion regulation, we can exert considerable control over the emotions and stress we feel in a few extremely effective ways:

➤ **The first strategy** is to change the parts of the world you expose yourself to. You can do this by moderating your use of social media, turning off the TV, not seeking out the goriest movies and staying away from the divisive forces in your life.

➤ **The second strategy** is to change your mental activity, either through attention or thinking. You can be exposed to something nasty, but you can shift your attention in a very rapid way so that you think of other things that are more positive or neutral. Say you're stuck in a meeting with people who are very toxic. You can develop the capacity to shift or modify your emotional focus, and that can be immensely powerful.

➤ **The third strategy** is to change your body and how it responds to stressors by using deep breathing or relaxation techniques to calm yourself.

To that end, the following are a roundup of breaks and buffers, proven strategies to create these all-important periods of low to no stress:

Exercise.

_____

One summer, I interviewed a group of high achievers—Twitter founder Biz Stone and *Kite Runner* author Khaled Hosseini among them—about their favorite ways to relieve stress. An overwhelming majority responded: "We exercise."

Indeed, physical activity increases oxygen circulation and bumps up the production of endorphins, both effects resulting in reduced stress and anxiety, and a greater sense of well-being. Exercising gives great bang for the buck. If (like me) you are reluctant to engage in hard activity, begin with something quick and relatively painless, like a brisk walk or slow bike ride around the block or a one-minute jump-roping session. Both will get your heart rate up quickly, and you can work your way up to more intense activities.

Take herbs.

_____

Naturopath and clinical nutritionist Dr. John Abdo recommends a few herbs proven to help reduce stress, such as rhodiola and ashwagandha. Both provide adrenal support for stress relief and bring a sense of calm, he says. Though Abdo considers both to be safe, you should always consult your doctor before taking supplements. Learn more about these and other herbs from the National Institutes of Health's National Center for Complementary and Alternative Medicine database (nccam.nih.gov).

Sniff some scents.

Research shows that inhaling essential oils can result in measurable changes in brain wave activity. According to Kathi Keville, aromatherapist and coauthor of *Aromatherapy: A Complete Guide to the Healing Art*, essential oils exert specific effects on both body and mind. Lavender and chamomile were once sewn into pillows to help people relax when they lay down. She recommends placing four drops of lavender or chamomile essential oil into a steaming pot of water or diffuser to scent your home. The scents can also be used together. Other therapeutic oils for relaxation include rose geranium and citruses, like orange and lemon.

Laugh.

Scientific studies confirm that laughter is a great stress reliever. Laughing causes physical changes: it activates endorphins, relaxes muscles, stimulates circulation and generally calms the stress response. If you are feeling particularly adventurous, you can join a laughter yoga class (there is such a thing). Or you can just laugh and skip the yoga.

Spend time in nature.

Spend an hour or two alone out in nature, walking and considering the sights and sounds, textures and smells. One ground rule: No technology. That includes music, cell phones or any other gadgets.

Hang out with a pet.

Pets help lower blood pressure, reduce stress hormones and enhance your sense of well-being. Studies have shown that pet owners report fewer sick days, sleep better and are generally more active.

Slow down time.

We experience time in a highly subjective way. Being more present by focusing on what you are doing, continuing to learn, meeting new people, visiting new places, trying new activities and generally doing things differently from the way you have done them before (even just by taking a different route to school or work or using a different hand to do chores!) help slow down the perception of time passing.

Sleep.

You have by now heard enough about the critical importance of sleep to health and well-being. Sleep deprivation can lead to a climb in cortisol and a rise in inflammation markers. The relationship goes both ways, however. A good night's sleep can help reduce the effects of stress.

Pray.

Research shows that people who are more religious or spiritual are better able to cope with stress. They also experience benefits to health and well-being.

Read a book, listen to music.

Research shows that reading for as little as six minutes can reduce stress levels by up to 68 percent. The same study showed that listening to music also works, slowing down the subjects' heart rate and easing muscle tension by 61 percent.

APPENDIX II

RESOURCES AND FURTHER READING

The following represents, in no particular order, a small (and eclectic) sample of books, videos, audio, Web sites, podcasts and other resources I highly recommend. The links are current as of December 2014.

- "This Is Water," a commencement speech about perception (and so much more) by David Foster Wallace, easily found on YouTube. I highly recommend hearing it in Foster Wallace's own voice, but you can also find transcripts of the talk.

- If you could have only one thing to read while stranded on a desert island, it would be Maria Popova's remarkable Brain Pickings: http://www.brainpickings.org/. Also peruse brainpicker's soundcloud: https://soundcloud.com/brainpicker

- *This American Life* [radio archives of some of the best stories of our lives]: http://www.thisamericanlife.org/

- The Moth: http://themoth.org/stories

- Scott Barry Kaufman's The Creativity Post: http://www
.creativitypost.com/

- Annie Murphy Paul's The Brilliant Blog: http://
anniemurphypaul.com/blog/

- The Unmistakable Creative Podcast [Candid conversations
with creative entrepreneurs and insanely interesting people]
http://unmistakablecreative.com/

- MessyNessyChic, a collection of the rare, unusual and
extraordinary things about our world: http://www
.messynessychic.com/

- David Shenk, *The Genius in All of Us.*

- Chip Heath and Dan Heath, *Switch: How to Change Things
When Change Is Hard*

- Eckhart Tolle, A New Earth podcasts with Oprah Winfrey

- SoulPancake YouTube channel: https://www.youtube.com/
user/soulpancake

- Filmmaker Joshua Homnick's Instagram, with glimpses into
moments of radical amazement found in everyday urban
environments: http://instagram.com/homnick

- Harvard Business Review: http://hbr.org/

- MIT Media Lab: http://www.media.mit.edu/

- MIT Technology Review: http://www.technologyreview.com/

- Stanford Graduate School of Business YouTube channel: https://www.youtube.com/user/stanfordbusiness

- Cognitive neuroscientist Andrea Kuszewski's Web site: www.andreakuszewski.com. Also, her fantastic Twitter feed: https://twitter.com/AndreaKuszewski

- Charles Duhigg, *The Power of Habit*

- Leo Babauta's Zen Habits blog: http://zenhabits.net/ and his book, *The Power of Less.*

- Daniel Pink, *A Whole New Mind*

- Kelly McGonigal's fantastic TED talk, How to Make Stress Your Friend: http://www.ted.com/talks/kelly_mcgonigal_how_to_make_stress_your_friend

- Videos from the Aspen Ideas Festival: http://www.aspenideas.org/

- Michael Pollan's books, *In Defense of Food* and *The Omnivore's Dilemma*

- Elizabeth Dunn and Michael Norton, *Happy Money: The Science of Smarter Spending*

- Paul Pitchford, *Healing with Whole Foods*

- Deepak Chopra, *The Seven Spiritual Laws of Success*

- Jalal al-Din Rumi, *The Essential Rumi* (translated by Coleman Barks)

- Daniel Kahneman, *Thinking, Fast and Slow*

- Nassim Nicholas Taleb, *Antifragile: Things That Gain from Disorder* and *The Black Swan*

- Author Elizabeth Gilbert's often-inspiring Facebook feed: https://www.facebook.com/GilbertLiz

- Michael Moss, *Salt Sugar Fat*

- Videos from the Being Human conferences: http://www.beinghuman.org/

- The Greater Good Science Center: http://greatergood.berkeley.edu/

- InsightLA guided meditations and Dharma talks: http://www.insightla.org/audio/

- The Authentic Happiness Web site at the University of Pennsylvania: https://www.authentichappiness.sas.upenn.edu/

- The Center for Compassion and Altruism Research and Education at Stanford blog and archives: http://ccare.stanford.edu/

- Jan Chozen Bays, *How to Train a Wild Elephant and Other Adventures in Mindfulness*

- Robert Sapolsky, *Why Zebras Don't Get Ulcers*

- Stanford d.school's bootcamp bootleg, "an active toolkit to support your design thinking practice": http://dschool .stanford.edu/wp-content/uploads/2011/03/ BootcampBootleg2010v2SLIM.pdf

- The Minimalists, a blog about living a meaningful life with less stuff: http://www.theminimalists.com/

- The Story of Stuff: http://storyofstuff.org/movies/story-of-stuff/ and the story of many other things, too: http:// storyofstuff.org/movies/

- Viktor E. Frankl, *Man's Search for Meaning*

- Sonja Lyubomirsky, *The How of Happiness*

- Caroline Myss, *Anatomy of the Spirit*

- Steven Pressfield, *The War of Art*

- Ryan Rigoli's Soulful Brand blogs and articles: http:// soulfulbrand.com/articles/

- NASA images, videos and podcasts: http://www.nasa .gov/

- Homa Sabet Tavangar, *Growing Up Global*

- Brandon Stanton's remarkable photograph series (and tribute to our essential belonging), "Humans of New York"

- Fiction! "Reading fiction is important," wrote the novelist Ann Patchett. "It is a vital means of imagining a life other than our own, which in turn makes us more empathetic beings."

SELECTED SOURCES

Listed below, by chapter, are the principal works referred to in the text, as well as others that supplied me with facts or influenced my thinking. Web site URLs are current as of October 2014. Any articles of mine cited here are available at amanda-enayati.com.

PART ONE
THE TRUE STORY OF STRESS

Chapter One • The Stories We Tell Ourselves

American Psychological Association's Stress in America survey: http://www.apa.org/news/press/releases/stress/.

Interview with Colum McCann at Aspen Summer Words. You can see McCann in a short video on the democracy of storytelling at: http://www.egs.edu/faculty/colum-mccann/videos/the-democracy-of-storytelling/.

NPR/Robert Wood Johnson Foundation/Harvard School of Public Health, The Burden of Stress in America, http://media.npr.org/documents/2014/july/npr_rwfj_harvard_stress_poll.pdf.

The Essential Rumi, Jalal al-Din Rumi, translated by Coleman Barks.

Alia J. Crum, Peter Salovey and Shawn Achor, "Rethinking Stress: The Role of Mindsets in Determining the Stress Response," *Journal of Personality and Social Psychology*, April 2013.

Also see Dr. Crum's fascinating talk about the influence of mindsets: TEDxTraverseCity 2014, "Alia Crum: Change Your Mindset, Change the Game," June 18, 2014, https://www.youtube.com/watch?v=ev65 KnPHVUk.

Chapter Two • The Most Trying Times

From my article "Don't Let Others Stress You Out," CNN Health, September 7, 2011.

Interview with Anne Harrington.

Anne Harrington, *The Cure Within*, and Harrington's lecture, "Culture May Affect How Bodies Function," at Being Human 2012, https://www .youtube.com/watch?v=MMS4zGoh4Qs.

Robert M. Sapolsky, "How to Relieve Stress," *Greater Good Science Center*, March 22, 2012. Do not miss the video clips of Sapolsky on this page.

Mark Jackson, *The Age of Stress: Science and the Search for Stability*.

Robert M. Sapolsky, *Why Zebras Don't Get Ulcers*.

Alex Spiegel, "The Secret History Behind the Science of Stress," NPR, July 7, 2014.

Hans Selye, *The Stress of My Life*.

Interview with Mark Petticrew.

M. P. Petticrew and K. Lee, "The 'Father of Stress' Meets 'Big Tobacco': Hans Selye and the Tobacco Industry," *American Journal of Public Health*, March 2011.

Chapter Three • The Power of Perception

From my article "The Power of Perceptions: Imagining the Reality You Want," CNN Health, April 14, 2012.

Beau Lotto's lecture, "Perception and Sensations," at Being Human 2012, http://fora.tv/2012/03/24/Being_Human_Perception_Sensations.

Beau Lotto, "Optical Illusions Show How We See," TEDGlobal 2009, http://www.ted.com/talks/beau_lotto_optical_illusions_show_how_we_see?language=en.

Interview with neuroscientist and artist Beau Lotto, founder of Lottolab.

Interview with sociologist Ruha Benjamin, Princeton University.

Charles M. Blow, "The Curious Case of Trayvon Martin," *New York Times*, March 17, 2012.

Viktor Frankl, *Man's Search for Meaning*.

Khalil Gibran, *The Prophet*.

"This Is Water," a stunning commencement address by the late David Foster Wallace, https://www.youtube.com/watch?v=8CrOL-ydFMI.

Chapter Four • The Physiology of Stress

From my article "The Vicious Physiology of Stress," CNN Health, November 16, 2011.

Interview with Rajita Sinha.

Interview with Lorenzo Cohen.

Yale Stress Center: http://yalestress.org/.

"Understanding the Stress Response," *Harvard Mental Health Letter*, March 2011.

Bryon Adinoff, Ali Iranmanesh, Johannes Veldhuis and Lisa Fisher, "Disturbances of the Stress Response," *National Institute on Alcohol Abuse and Alcoholism*, 1998.

Robert M. Sapolsky, "How to Relieve Stress," *Greater Good Science Center*, March 22, 2012.

Alia J. Crum, Peter Salovey and Shawn Achor, "Rethinking Stress: The Role of Mindsets in Determining the Stress Response," *Journal of Personality and Social Psychology*, April 2013.

Kristin Sainani, "What, Me Worry?" *Stanford Magazine*, May/June 2014.

Firdaus Dhabhar's TED Talk: "The Positive Effects of Stress," https://www.youtube.com/watch?v=nsc83N-Q1q4.

See Sheldon Cohen, Denise Janicki-Deverts, William J. Doyle, Gregory E. Miller, Ellen Frank, Bruce S. Rabin, and Ronald B. Turner, "Chronic Stress, Glucocorticoid Receptor Resistance, Inflammation, and Disease Risk," *Proceedings of the National Academy of Sciences*, April 2012.

Ray Hainer, "Loneliness Hurts the Heart," CNN Health, August 10, 2009.

From my article "How to Stop Kids from Stressing," CNN Health, February 16, 2012.

Interview with Conor Liston.

Chapter Five • A New Narrative

From my article "Thrive Under Pressure Like a Pro Athlete," CNN Health, November 2, 2011.

Interview with Rajita Sinha, Ruha Benjamin, Michael Gervais.

M. Scott Peck, *The Road Less Traveled.*

Robert Frost, "A Servant to Servants."

Michael Rosen, *We're Going on a Bear Hunt.*

Jerome Groopman, *The Anatomy of Hope.*

PART TWO
STRESS AS A GUIDE

Introduction to Part Two • The New Rules

W. H. Auden, *The Age of Anxiety: A Baroque Eclogue.*

Daniel Smith, "It's Still the Age of Anxiety. Or Is It?," *New York Times,* January 14, 2012.

Chapter Six • Your World

Rule 1 • *Be Resilient*
From my articles "How Words Have the Power to Heal," CNN Health, June 29, 2011.

"Dealing with a Different Trip: The Guilt Trip," CNN Health, December 12, 2012.

"After Trauma, Teaching Hope," CNN Health, August 19, 2011.

"Steps to Help You Thrive in Hard Times," CNN Health, August 24, 2011.

James W. Pennebaker, *Writing to Heal: A Guided Journal for Recovering from Trauma and Emotional Upheaval.*

Emilia Lahti, "Words Making Our Worlds: Introducing Sisu," *The Creativity Post*, June 5, 2014.

Martin Seligman, "Building Resilience," *Harvard Business Review*, April 2011.

Karen Reivich, *The Resilience Factor.*

Penn Resiliency Program, www.ppc.sas.upenn.edu/prpsum.htm.

Penn's VIA Survey of Character Strengths (and a number of other related tests) by registering for free at www.authentichappiness.com.

James W. Pennebaker and Cindy K. Chung, *Expressive Writing: Connections to Physical and Mental Health.*

Interviews with Martin Seligman, James Pennebaker, Karen Reivich, Rhonda Cornum, Emilia Lahti, James Tagney, Chris Klug, Nancy Morgan.

Rule 2 · Belong

From my articles "The Importance of Belonging," CNN Health, June 1, 2012.

"Fighting Loneliness and Disease with Meditation," CNN Health, August 25, 2012.

"The Powers of Perception: Imaging the Reality You Want," CNN Health, April 14, 2012.

"Is There a Bias Against Civility," CNN Health, March 28, 2012.

Marina Keegan, "The Opposite of Loneliness," *Yale News*, May 27, 2012.

Interviews with Gregory Walton, David Creswell.

John Cacioppo, *Lonelines: Human Nature and the Need for Social Connection.*

Also see Gregory Walton, "Encouraging a Sense of Belonging," Stanford Graduate School of Business, May 10, 2012, https://www.youtube.com/watch?v=--9xzUxOxpU.

Jill Bolte-Taylor, *My Stroke of Insight.*

Kahlil Gibran, *The Collected Works.*

Annie Murphy Paul, "A Group Doesn't Even Have to Exist to Affect Our Behavior," Brilliant Blog, April 25, 2013, http://anniemurphypaul.com/2013/04/a-group-doesnt-even-have-to-exist-to-affect-our-behavior/#.

Annie Murphy Paul's The Brilliant Blog, anniemurphypaul.com/blog/

Rule 3 · Be Creative

David Kelley's TED talk, "How to Build Your Creative Confidence," www.ted.com/talks/david_kelley_how_to_build_your_creative_confidence.

Interviews with Fernando Pullum, David Kelley, Beau Lotto, Jennifer Mueller, Susan Ochs, Laura Richardson, Ruha Benjamin.

Beau Lotto's TED talk, "Optical Illusions Show How We See," www.ted.com/talks/beau_lotto_optical_illusions_show_how_we_see.

Do not miss Maria Popova's brilliant blog, Brain Pickings, "a subjective lens on what matters in the world and why,": www.brainpickings.org.

Rule 4 · Be Free

From my articles "The Aging Brain: Why Getting Older Just Might Be Awesome," CNN Health, June 19, 2012.

"A Creative Life Is a Healthy Life," CNN Health, May 26, 2012.

Interview with Tony Schwartz. Schwartz has identified six keys to achieving excellence—and letting go of stasis—at any age: pursue what you love, do the hardest work first, practice intensely, seek expert feedback in intermittent doses, take regular renewal breaks and ritualize practice. Read the article at http://blogs.hbr.org/2010/08/six-keys-to-being-excellent-at. Also check out his fantastic blog, The Energy Project at: http://theenergyproject.com/.

Interviews with Shilloy Sanchez, David Kelley, Kathleen Taylor, Debra Dunn, Gary Small, Tony Wagner.

Steven Pressfield, *The War of Art*.

Deepak Chopra, *The Seven Spiritual Laws of Success*.

Susan M. Ochs, *Inside the Banker's Brain: Mental Models in the Financial Services Industry and Implications for Consumers, Practitioners and Regulators*, June 2014.

Interview with Susan Ochs.

Interview with Laura Richardson, principal designer, Frog Design.

Oprah Winfrey, Master Class, http://www.oprah.com/own-master-class/Oprah-Winfreys-Master-Class-Quotes.

David Shenk, *The Genius in All of Us*.

IDEO, design thinking blog, http://designthinking.ideo.com/.

MIT Media Lab, http://www.media.mit.edu/.

Stanford d.school's human-centered design, "The Bootcamp Bootleg," http://dschool.stanford.edu/wp-content/uploads/2011/03/BootcampBootleg2010v2SLIM.pdf.

Chapter Seven   •   Your Mind

Rule 5   •   Be Happy

Eduardo Porter, *The Price of Everything.*

M. Scott Peck, *The Road Less Traveled.*

Daniel Kahneman, *Thinking, Fast and Slow.*

Philip Moeller, "Why Seeking More Money Hurts Happiness," *U.S. News & World Report*, April 9, 2012.

Interviews with Jean Twenge and Tim Kasser.

Jean Twenge, *Generation Me.*

Center on the Developing Child, Harvard University, www.developing child.harvard.edu/.

Elizabeth W. Dunn and Michael Norton, "Don't Indulge. Be Happy," *New York Times*, July 7, 2012.

Emily Esfahani Smith's fantastic writing in *The Atlantic*, including "There's More to Life Than Being Happy," *The Atlantic*, January 9, 2013, and "Meaning Is Healthier than Happiness," *The Atlantic*, August 1, 2013.

The United Nations International Day of Happiness Web site, www.dayof happiness.net.

Roy F. Baumeister, Kathleen D. Vohs, Jennifer L. Aaker and Emily N. Garbinsky, "Some Key Differences Between a Happy Life and a Meaningful Life," *Journal of Positive Psychology*, August 20, 2013.

The Greater Good Science Center, based at the University of California, Berkeley, contains a wealth of material on the science and practice of social and emotional well-being: http://greatergood.berkeley.edu/.

Rule 6 · Be Giving

From my articles "Stress May Be Causing Your Cravings," CNN Health, May 23, 2012.

"For Kids, It's Better to Give Than Receive," CNN Living, September 17, 2012.

Interviews with Jim McDermott, Elizabeth Dunn, Lara B. Aknin and J. Kiley Hamlin, Dr. Jan Chozen Bays, Lee Klinger Lesser.

Elizabeth W. Dunn and Michael Norton, "Don't Indulge. Be Happy," *New York Times*, July 7, 2012.

Elizabeth Dunn and Michael Norton, *Happy Money: The Science of Smarter Spending*.

J. Quoidbach, E. W. Dunn, K. V. Petrides and M. Mikolajczak, "Money Giveth, Money Taketh Away: The Dual Effect of Wealth on Happiness," *Psychological Science*, May 2010.

E. L. Deci, R. Koestner and R. Ryan, "A Meta-Analytic Review of Experiments Examining the Effects of Extrinsic Rewards on Intrinsic Motivations," *Psychological Bulletin*, November 1999.

"How Rewards Can Backfire and Reduce Motivation," PsyBlog, October 12, 2009, www.spring.org.uk/2009/10/how-rewards-can-backfire-and-reduce-motivation.php.

John Tierney, "How to Win the Lottery (Happily)," *New York Times*, May 26, 2014.

See also Lara B. Aknin, J. Kiley Hamlin and Elizabeth W. Dunn, "Giving Leads to Happiness in Young Children," *PLoS ONE*, 2012.

Jan Chozen Bays, *How to Train a Wild Elephant and Other Adventures in Mindfulness*.

Rule 7 · Be Kind

From my article "Don't Let Others Stress You Out," CNN Health, September 7, 2011.

Interviews with Daniel Goleman, Elaine Hatfield, Daniel Rempala, Pamela Casey, James Gross, Piero Forni, Trudy Goodman and Robert Sutton.

Dorothy Foltz-Gray, "How Contagious Are Your Emotions?," *O, The Oprah Magazine*, December 2004.

Arlene R. Gordon Research Institute, New York.

Amanda Chan, "Yes, Your Stress Really Is Rubbing Off on Everyone Around You," Huffington Post, May 5, 2014.

Piero Forni, *The Civility Solution: What to Do When People Are Rude.*

A. Kramer, J. Guillory and J. Hancock, "Experimental Evidence of Massive Scale Emotional Contagion Through Social Networks," *Proceedings of the National Academy of Sciences*, June 17, 2014.

Elizabeth Gilbert's Facebook post on her loving-kindness meditation practice, https://www.facebook.com/GilbertLiz/photos/a.356148997800555.79726.227291194019670/712136635535121/?type=1.

"Greater Happiness in Five Minutes a Day," Greater Good Science Center, September 10, 2012, http://greatergood.berkeley.edu/raising_happiness/post/better_than_sex_and_appropriate_for_kids.

Chapter Eight   •   Your Body

Rule 8   •   Be Healthy

From my articles "Stress May Be Causing Your Cravings," CNN Health, May 23, 2013.

"Avoid the Afternoon Stress Eating Binge," CNN Health, February 8, 2012.

"Habits—Good and Bad—Stick When You're Stressed," CNN Health, June 26, 2013.

Michael Pollan, *In Defense of Food: An Eater's Manifesto.*

Michael Pollan, *The Omnivore's Dilemma.*

Tyler G. Graham and Drew Ramsey, *The Happiness Diet.*

Sarah-Marie Hopf, "You Are What You Eat: How Food Affects Your Mood," *Dartmouth Undergraduate Journal of Science*, February 3, 2011.

Interview with Robin Kenarek, Manuel Villacorta, Rajita Sinha, Brandon Marcello, David Neal, Hemi Weingarten.

Charles M. Duhigg, *The Power of Habit.*

Michael Moss, *Salt, Sugar, Fat.*

You can read more about Stanford Performance Dining categories here: https://www.google.com/webhp?sourceid=chrome-instant&ion =1&espv=2&ie=UTF-8#safe=active&q=stanford%20performance %20dining.

The Fooducate blog, http://blog.fooducate.com/.

Gardiner Harris, "F.D.A. Panel to Consider Warnings for Artificial Food Colorings," *New York Times*, March 29, 2011.

"What Is Mindfulness?," Greater Good Science Center, http://greater good.berkeley.edu/topic/mindfulness/definition.

Rule 9 · *Be Uncluttered*

From my article "Seeking Serenity: A Life Less Cluttered," CNN Health, June 16, 2011.

Interviews with Leo Babauta, Ryan Rigoli and Mikael Cho.

Leo Babauta, *The Power of Less*, and his blog, Zen Habits, at http://zen habits.net/.

Ryan Rigoli's Soulful Brand blog, http://soulfulbrand.com/articles/.

Sex, Lies and Videotape, directed by Steven Soderbergh.

Mikael Cho, "How Clutter Affects Your Brain (and What You Can Do About It)," *Lifehacker*, July 5, 2013.

Stephanie McMains and Sabine Kastner, "Interactions of Top-Down and Bottom-Up Mechanisms in Human Visual Cortex," *The Journal of Neuroscience*, January 12, 2011.

Mark Hurst, *Bit Literacy*.

The Minimalists blog, http://www.theminimalists.com/.

Gretchen Rubin, The Happiness Project.

Gretchen Rubin, "Good Stuff," *New York Times*, August 18, 2012.

The Story of Stuff Project, which includes a fantastic short documentary about the life cycle of material goods, http://storyofstuff.org.

Chapter Nine · World, Mind and Body

Rule 10 · Be Present

From my article "Seeking Serenity: When Lawyers Go Zen," CNN Health, May 11, 2011.

Tyger Latham, "The Depressed Lawyer," *Psychology Today*, May 2, 2011.

Interviews with Bob Roth, Charles Halpern, Doug Chermak.

Deepak Chopra, "Sleep and Meditation," www.deepakchopra.com/blog/view/1613/sleep_and_meditation.

"Kenneth Branagh's Aha! Moment: How I Learned to Meditate," *O, The Oprah Magazine*, May 2011.

Martin Boroson's one-moment meditation, www.youtube.com/watch?v=F6eFFCi12v8.

Jack Kornfield, *The Wise Heart*.

Jon Kabat-Zinn is the founder of the Center for Mindfulness in Medicine, Health Care and Society, as well as the Stress Reduction Clinic, at the University of Massachusetts Medical School. More information about Kabat-Zinn's mindful-based stress reduction can be found here: www.mindfullivingprograms.com/whatMBSR.php.

ACKNOWLEDGMENTS

Two short years after my scrape with cancer, when my steps forward were hesitant and wobbly, I began to write a blog. I named it "Practical Magic for Beginners," and through it I sought to rewrite a life story I thought had gone desperately wrong thus far. An army of angels came to support, to cheer, to lend a hand. Some of them I knew already and some I came to know and love through their words and spirits. They were so magical to me that I gave them titles: the Force of Nature, the Sage, the Columnist and so many more. I want to thank these women and men first, because they gave me power at a time when I had very little of my own. I want to extend my love and gratitude to: Blanca Uzeta O'Leary (a true force of nature), Juan R. Palomo, LaToya Baldwin Clark, Chitra Badii, Molly Bates Efrusy, Kanwar Singh, Larissa Lockyer Baker, John Black and Toiya Black, Michele Mason, Jane Sheffield Lowery, Lydia Boroughs, Iris Bunim, Jay Gilbertson, Jaleh Sluis, Aane Vonk, Clara Cristofaro, Ana White, Marnie Pope Bermingham, Maricela Pappas, Judy Hanson Boyd, Cavanaugh O'Leary . . . and so many others. Your love made me bold and audacious.

A world of thanks to Arianna Huffington, Erica Jong and Charles Duhigg, and to friends—near, far and virtual—who inspire and delight every day: Bill Resnick, Michael Stubbs and Winnie Resnick, Rajita Sinha, Lynn Hirshfield, Bob Roth, Janis Minton, Fernando Pullum, Ryan Rigoli, Jim McDermott and Deb Cincotta, Jody and Malik Sievers, Ruha Benjamin, Jehmu Greene, Victoria Zackheim, Tim Kasser, Emilia Lahti, Andrea

Kuszewski, Renea Frey, Scott Barry Kaufman, Judith Orloff, Joshua Homnick, Pamela Casey, Jace Alexander Casey, Mari Soberg, Arya Badiyan, Shilloy Sanchez, Sarah Granger, Lisen Stromberg, Hemi Weingarten, Joel and Kathryn Bass, Kathy Etemad, Ethan Zindler, Harry Weiner, Michelle Beaty, Jamie Craig, John Russo, Liz Dwyer, Judy Martin, Deb Crawford, Kristin Carlson, Kerah Cottrell and Lucy Donovan, Nishat and Pieter Ruiter, Pam Cloyd Lighaam, Homa Sabet Tavangar, Joanne Capper, Christopher and Jennifer Gandin Le, Tatiana Zamir, Laurie Sobel and Leisa McNeese, Deb Crawford, Judith Hammerman, Manuel Villacorta, Duane Bidwell, Muni Tahzib, Chris Cogley, Claire Noble, Jennifer Sullivan Corkern, Najeeba Syeed, Parisa Banks and Chitra Golestani Maghzi, Courtney Gabrielle Restivo, Wendy Maldonado, Brittany and Caitlin O'Grady, Arielle Kasindi, Nikhil Goyal, Susan Ochs, Mimi Ramirez, Michael Gervais, Shannon Jacobs English, Thangam Chandrasekaran and Yesh Subramanian, Frank Robinson and Stephanie Jaczko Robinson and Allissa Ackerman Robinson.

My gratitude to Sarah Hepola for finding and running that first Salon story that transformed my narrative from "Why always me?" to "Bring it on."

Christa Robinson: Thank you for opening that door, dear friend.

There are people out in the world whose divine threads show up, again and again, in others' life tapestries. Mary Carter: How can I ever thank you enough?

I have had the very good fortune of working with the gifted Jacque Wilson for years.

The fierce and wise Brandi Bowles, who came to me through Practical Magic.

The brilliant and formidable crew of women at CNN Health through the years: Ashley Estes Hayes, Liz Landau, Jennifer Seitz.

The amazing Jen Schuster of Penguin.

My supremely creative brother-friend, Dave Anderson.

The folks at Aspen Summer Words, Aspen Ideas Festival and the amazing women at EWIP.

Maman, Baba, Hamid, Noushin, Nina, Sarah and Amy, and Bahar, Bas and Vahid.

And first, last and always: Jaime, Mina and Rohan.

INDEX